HC260.
W4 MOR

QM Library
23 1309800 2

THE STRUCTURE OF PROPERTY OWNERSHIP IN GREAT BRITAIN

WITHDRAWN
FROM STOCK
QMUL LIBRARY

THE STRUCTURE OF PROPERTY OWNERSHIP IN GREAT BRITAIN

BY

E. VICTOR MORGAN

OXFORD
AT THE CLARENDON PRESS
1960

Oxford University Press, Amen House, London E.C.4
GLASGOW NEW YORK TORONTO MELBOURNE WELLINGTON
BOMBAY CALCUTTA MADRAS KARACHI KUALA LUMPUR
CAPE TOWN IBADAN NAIROBI ACCRA

© *Oxford University Press 1960*

11480
KJ100
C

PRINTED IN GREAT BRITAIN

QUEEN MARY COLLEGE
LIBRARY
MILE END ROAD
LONDON, E.1.

PREFACE

THE studies on which this book is based were made possible by a grant from the Social Studies Research Fund of the University College of Swansea, which enabled me to have the help of Mrs. E. J. Cleary as research assistant. The work owes an enormous amount to her skill and zeal, and I should like to record my gratitude both to her and to the College. Information was obtained from published sources listed in the bibliography, from the study of a large number of balance-sheets, and from questionnaires. The number of people who helped either by giving us access to accounts or by answering questions runs into thousands; a few of them are mentioned by name in the text, but I should like to thank them all for the kindness and patience with which they treated my inquiries. I am also very grateful to Miss Cynthia Taylor (now Mrs. E. Tull), Mrs. M. Tyrrell, and Mrs. J. Charles for the help they gave me while they were working, successively, as computers in the Economics Department, and to the Clarendon Press for their kindness and efficiency in dealing with a work which, by the nature of the material, must have given them trouble disproportionate to its length.

The estimates of ownership given here vary considerably in accuracy between different sectors and different types of asset, and an attempt has been made to indicate likely sources of error in the text. In some cases more accurate estimates are, theoretically, obtainable, though only at a prohibitive cost. In others, nothing more can be done until there are changes either in the law or in the attitudes of institutions towards the release of information under their control. Such changes are, however, happening, and new pieces of evidence are continually becoming available. In some directions, the work of the Radcliffe Committee has brought a notable acceleration of this process. The manuscript of this book was completed before the publication of the *Radcliffe Report*; a few references to it have been inserted, but it was not possible to make a complete revision in the light both of the *Report* and the minutes of evidence.

E. VICTOR MORGAN

Swansea
April 1960

CONTENTS

LIST OF TABLES

Note. Figures, both for totals and individual items are normally given to the nearest £ million. Totals may, therefore, differ slightly from the sum of items due to rounding errors.

1

THE CONCEPT OF NATIONAL WEALTH DEFINITIONS AND METHODS OF VALUATION

ATTEMPTS to measure the value of the national capital can be traced back to the very early days of economic inquiry. Gregory King is best known for his estimate of the national income but the *Natural and Political Observations and Conclusions* (written in 1696) also contains an estimate of the value of the nation's capital. King estimates the value of land and buildings at £234 m. on a basis of eighteen years' purchase of their rent; capital employed in 'trades arts and labours' is put at £330 million, and liquid capital, in which King includes coin and bullion and also livestock, at £86 m.[1]

In the second quarter of the nineteenth century G. R. Porter devoted a section of his famous work *The Progress of the Nation* to what he called 'accumulation'.[2] In the course of this, Porter uses both the capitalization of income method (starting from assessment for rates and the early income-tax returns) and the method of estimating capital values from the legacy duty returns. On the second basis he estimated private property in 1845 at £2,200 m. He also quotes the figures of fire insurances as an indicator of the value of real property. Unfortunately, however, Porter's discussion of method is slight, and he makes no real attempt to reconcile his sources one with another.

Sir Robert Giffen is generally given the credit for making the first systematic use of the income-tax statistics in a paper presented to the Royal Statistical Society in 1878.[3] His estimate of the national capital was £8,548 m. The paper remains

[1] King quoted by Colin Clark, *National Income and Outlay*, Macmillan & Co., London, 1938, p. 217.

[2] G. R. Porter, *The Progress of the Nation*, 3rd ed., John Murray, London, 1857, pp. 588–629.

[3] Printed in *Essays on Finance*, George Bell & Sons, London, 1882.

interesting both for the discussion of method and for its statement of the uses of statistics of the national capital, a part of which deserves quotation.

> It is one of the means of taking stock of national progress or the reverse. We compare at different times the numbers of the population and the amounts of crime and pauperism in a country as some test of its moral progress; or the numbers of the population and particulars of certain home and foreign trades, or of the consumption of certain articles, as a test of material progress. In the same way we may compare the population at different times with the accumulated wealth or the rate of increase of population with the rate of increase of wealth as a test of progress, partly moral and partly material. The particular advantage of this last comparison will also be that it answers directly some important public questions as to what the margin of taxation is in a country, and whether and how much it is increasing or diminishing.

The systematic use of the estate duty statistics came much later, for it was not until 1908 that Sir B. Mallet gave his paper to the Royal Statistical Society on 'A Method of Estimating Capital Wealth from the Estate Duty Statistics'.[1] During the inter-war period both the income and estate methods were used, among others, by Lord Stamp and Mr. (now Sir Harry) Campion,[2] and there was a considerable amount of discussion of definition and methods. This discussion was partly concerned with statistical pitfalls in using the sources, and partly with more fundamental problems of definition. One of the most troublesome of the latter was how to treat obligations such as the national debt, which are regarded as wealth by their holders, but which are clearly not capital from the point of view of the nation as a whole.

Looking at the matter with the benefit of hindsight much of the difficulty over definitions seems to result from the search for a single concept of national capital which could be applied to any of a number of uses. Lord Stamp gives a list of the uses

[1] *J.R.S.S.*, 1908.

[2] Stamp, *British Incomes and Property*, P. S. King, London, 1927, and *The National Capital*, P. S. King, London, 1937. Campion, *Public and Private Property in Great Britain*, Oxford University Press, 1939.

of these statistics in which he amplifies the statement of Giffen already quoted.

1. Tests of 'progress' by way of comparisons between different years, to show the accumulation of capital; tests of the distribution of wealth, according to the form of embodiment which wealth takes; of the effects of changes in the rate of interest or in the value of money.
2. Tests of the relative 'prosperity' or resources of different nations or communities, either as a whole or per head of the population, and in relation to their national debts.
3. Comparisons of income with capital and property.
4. Considerations of the distribution of wealth according to individual fortunes, and changes in that distribution.
5. Considerations of the applicability and yield of schemes of taxation, e.g. the capital levy.
6. Questions relating to war indemnities.

After experience of trying to collect reparations, most economists would now hold that there were other factors far more important than the value of a country's capital in determining its capacity to pay war indemnities. The rest of Stamp's uses are still relevant and important, though sometimes his phraseology is different from that of the modern economist. For example, 'capital output ratios' are now more familiar tools than 'comparison of income with capital and property'.

Recent theoretical developments, however, suggest several additions to Stamp's list. Modern monetary theory regards the propensity of individuals and institutions to spend as capable of being influenced both by the amount of their property or net worth and by its liquidity, so that a knowledge both of the value and the type of property owned by various sectors of a community is important from this point of view.

The study of the inter-related assets and liabilities of different sectors of the community provides important information about the capital market and, ideally, studies of capital could be integrated with a 'flow of funds' analysis. If an appropriate and consistent basis of valuation is chosen, changes in the value of a particular asset held by a person or institution between any two dates will be equal to net expenditure on, or receipts from sales of that asset during the period between the two accounting dates. Thus, if enough information were available, the flow of funds between different sectors of the economy could be traced either through records of actual transactions or by taking the changes between periodical valuations. In practice, however, both the collection of information in sufficient detail and the use of an appropriate method of valuation offer serious difficulties.

These last three uses require not a single estimate of national capital, but a set of integrated statements for each important sector of the economy showing its real assets, its claims on each of the other sectors, and its liabilities to them. Such a set of integrated balance-sheets is a logical complement to the integrated income and expenditure account with which we have become familiar during the past fifteen years. A number of writers have discussed the general principle constructing such an integrated statement of assets and liabilities;[1] in America the matter has been taken considerably further and, thanks to the pioneering work of Dr. Raymond W. Goldsmith, a great deal of the relevant statistics have been compiled and related to one another. In Britain, however, though there have been several post-war estimates of national capital, no integrated statement of assets and liabilities has yet been published. It is this gap that the present study was mainly designed to fill. Such a project has, however, to face a number of problems both of definition and valuation.

It is possible to distinguish between a number of different concepts of 'capital' each of which is valid for certain purposes. The following seem to be important:

(*a*) The total value of the real assets physically situated in a country, including assets owned by non-residents and excluding residents' holdings of foreign assets. This would be the concept

[1] J. R. Hicks, *The Social Framework*, 2nd ed., Oxford University Press, 1952, appendix D; A. T. Peacock and H. C. Edey, *National Income and Social Accounting*, Nisbet, London, and Cambridge University Press, 1954, and Raymond W. Goldsmith, 'The National Balance Sheet of the U.S.A., 1900–49' in *Income and Wealth*, series iv, Bowes & Bowes, London, 1955.

of capital appropriate, for example, to comparisons of capital with income or output. Fixed capital, stocks and work in progress should obviously be included, but there is some difficulty about the treatment of land and natural resources. For practical purposes it is virtually impossible to separate the value of land from that of the capital embodied in improvements. Where developed land is used for an economic purpose it is rightly regarded as an asset by the person or institution owning it, and it seems best to include its value as part of the national capital. Undeveloped natural resources, which as yet have no market value, should not be recorded, though they are often vaguely referred to as part of the national wealth.

(*b*) The real assets owned by residents in (or for some purposes citizens of) a country. This differs from (*a*) in excluding real assets located in the country but owned by non-residents, and including similar assets owned by residents but located abroad. Financial claims on non-residents should also be included and a corresponding deduction should be made for financial obligations to non-residents. An internal financial claim constitutes a liability of one person or institution and an asset of another, and both the payment of interest and the redemption of the debt involve only internal transfers, and make no difference to the total real assets of the community. A financial claim on a non-resident does, however, enable the community as a whole to add to it real income and so these claims deserve to be included.

A special point arises here in connexion with the money stock. Obviously token coin or paper money should either not be counted at all or, at most, be given a value equal only to their cost of production. On the other hand, coin made of the precious metals and monetary reserves held in bullion can always be used to acquire real assets from abroad. In this way, they are analogous to financial claims on non-residents, and they should, therefore, be included.

The total of real assets owned by residents, net financial claims on non-residents and monetary stocks of the precious metals corresponds most closely with national wealth in the sense in which those words are generally used. It would be the appropriate concept, for example, for historical studies of capital accumulation and for comparisons of wealth between one country and another.

(*c*) A very different but also important concept is that of private net worth. While a debt owned by an individual or a bond or share of a company form an asset of one unit and a liability of another, and so cancel out on aggregation, the government debt forms a private asset against which there is no corresponding private liability. The debt is obviously not part of the national wealth, but holdings of it are part of the assets of individual units, and the amount and type of their holdings will influence their economic decisions. If one is considering asset holdings as an influence on the behaviour of the private sector, one must, therefore, include holdings of the debt, and we define private net worth as the sum of real assets and net financial claims on foreigners owned by the private sector plus its net holdings of the liabilities of public bodies.

(*d*) Finally, there is the concept of private gross worth which would be simply the sum of private assets, real and financial, without allowing for liabilities. This would, of course, involve a great deal of double counting, and is of very limited usefulness. There is one context however, in which it is of some slight interest. When an asset is owned directly by the ultimate beneficiary, it would appear only once in the total of gross worth, and there is no double counting. When it is owned indirectly, e.g. a share in a joint-stock company, it appears twice—in the assets of the holder and in the balance-sheet of the company. Sometimes, of course, there are several links in the chain between the legal owner and the ultimate beneficiary, and then an asset appears several times over. This divorce of legal owner from ultimate beneficiary tends to become more prevalent as the economic and financial system develops, and the change over time in the ratio of gross to net worth gives a rough index of this development.

Turning to the method of valuation we may suggest a number of conditions which an ideal system should fulfil:

(*a*) the value assigned to any asset should be that which is most meaningful to the holder;

(*b*) values should be consistent in that the same value is put on an asset regardless of the sector in which it is owned;

(*c*) valuation of different types of asset should be consistent in that, when balance-sheets for a number of units (or sectors) are combined the items which represent claims of one such unit on another should cancel out, and the residue should give a true statement of the net worth of the group. If consolidation were carried to its logical conclusion and all balance-sheets in the community were consolidated this sort of consistency should entail that the residue would be a measure of national wealth; and

(*d*) values should be such as to permit net expenditure on assets during a period to be derived from changes in asset values, and so allow capital accounts to be integrated with flow of funds studies.

Unfortunately, not all these demands are reconcilable one with another even in theory and the gulf between what is theoretically desirable and what is practically possible is a wide one.

Once a real asset has been created, it is usually specific and has little use outside the purpose it was designed to serve. Its earnings, therefore, depend on the demand for its particular service and the supply of co-operant factors, and they are a quasi-rent. The economic theorist would, therefore, regard the value of such an asset as the present value of the series of annuities represented by the quasi-rents which the asset is expected to earn over the period of its prospective life.

Value in this sense could be estimated either by taking earnings over a given period and capitalizing them at whatever number of years purchase is considered appropriate, or by estimating actual market values. The former is the result achieved by estimates of national wealth derived primarily from the income-tax statistics, while the latter is the result of working from estate duty statistics. Neither score very good marks when tested against our theoretical criteria. The use of earnings suffers from the defects that actual earnings over a given short period may be very different from prospective earnings over the whole life of an asset, and that the choice of a number of years' purchase (with its implied rate of interest) is rather arbitrary; moreover, capitalized earnings is a concept that has very little meaning from the point of view of the owner of an asset. The use of market values suffers from the fact that both the market's estimate of earnings and the rate at which they are discounted are very volatile. Moreover, where the market value of the real asset has to be inferred from that of a share, the value of the share may be affected by considerations other than earnings, e.g. by a company's policy with regard to the proportion of its earnings paid out in dividends. Market value is more meaningful to the holder of an asset than capitalized earnings, but it does not seem likely that owners of business assets pay much attention to it.

Neither capitalized earnings nor market values bear any close relationship to the value of the financial liabilities which may be the counterpart of real assets, so that they would not fulfil our requirement (*c*), and neither would lend itself to incorporation into a flow of funds system.

The alternative is to value real assets either at historical cost less depreciation (which is the normal accounting practice) or at replacement cost. The difficulty about both is that they ignore the fact that investment may be ill-conceived or that changes in economic circumstances may deprive it of earning opportunities which might reasonably have been expected. In this case, valuation based on historical cost is of only historical interest, and valuation on replacement cost, not even that; the cost of replacing something that no one wants to replace is a very academic notion.

Values based on historical cost have the advantage of following general accounting practice, so that they are probably the most meaningful from the point of view of the holder. They also give a high degree of consistency between the value of real assets and financial liabilities and so reduce problems of consolidation to a minimum. Even here, however, there may be a hidden inconsistency, for the rate at which an asset is depreciated is bound to be rather arbitrary, and probably firms err on the side of caution and generally write off their assets before they have reached the end of their useful life. Firms behaving in this way would, of course, accumulate hidden reserves and a set of consolidated balance-sheets would understate national wealth to the extent of these hidden reserves.

So long as the investment concerned is yielding a 'normal' return, the replacement value of capital is the concept which lends itself most readily to some forms of economic analysis, particularly that of relation between capital and income, and this is probably the reason for the recent upsurge of interest in a replacement-cost valuation. It is, however, a most difficult thing to estimate, since owners rarely if ever have occasion to make direct estimates of replacement cost.[1] In the absence of a satisfactory direct estimate, the only alternative is to divide assets into categories, assume a length of life for each, estimate investment year by year over the whole life span, and revalue at current prices (allowing of course for depreciation). This was the basis of Mr. P. Redfern's method[2] but there are great difficulties in deciding the length of life one should assume, in estimating investment over a long period of history, and in obtaining reliable and relevant information about prices. A replacement-cost valuation does not, of course, lend itself to consolidation, and does not fit into a flow of funds analysis.

We have thus four methods of valuation: capitalized earnings, market value, original cost less depreciation, and replacement cost. As we have seen, each is different from the others and each has its own significance, but nevertheless they are more closely related than might at first appear.

In order to investigate this relationship further, let us first

[1] The most likely occasion for making such an estimate is for insurance purposes, and insurance figures have been used by Dr. T. Barna, 'The Replacement Cost of Fixed Assets on British Manufacturing Industry in 1955', *J.R.S.S.*, 1957, pp. 1–47.

[2] P. Redfern, 'Net Investment in Fixed Assets in the United Kingdom, 1938–53', ibid., 1955, pp. 141–82.

assume constant prices, so that it becomes unnecessary to distinguish between historical cost and replacement cost, and we can use the one word, cost. We assume also that there is a 'normal' rate of return on any particular type of asset, such that if earnings, as a percentage of cost, are persistently above the norm, the stock will be increased and earnings reduced through new investment. Similarly, if the rate of return falls significantly below the norm, the capital stock will be reduced through failure to make good depreciation until earnings are raised to normal. There will thus be a tendency for earnings as a proportion of cost to conform to this normal basis, though where the normal relationship is upset by any large disturbance its restoration may take a long time.

In statistical work based on the capitalization of income, a normal yield has, of course, to be estimated from actual yields. It seems reasonable to assume, however, that the average of actual yields over a number of years will give a fairly close approximation to the normal. A valuation reached in this way may, however, differ from cost for the following reasons:

1. For particular assets because they were particularly well or ill conceived, because they are more or less than averagely well managed, or because they have enjoyed good or bad luck in some way which has affected their earnings. In considering a large number of assets, however, such deviations may be expected to cancel out.

2. For groups of similar assets (a trade or industry) because the normal relationship has been upset by changes in the demand for the particular service that they render. In so far as these changes are only temporary fluctuations, they will cancel out if we take an average value over several years. They may, however, result from long-run trends in demand such that normal earnings can only be restored by major changes in the stock of capital. Even so, however, if we are considering the economy as a whole, we may expect that low capital values in declining industries will be balanced by high capital values in expanding industries, so that a considerable amount of cancelling out will still occur.

3. In particular short periods because fluctuations in the general level of activity cause earnings as a whole to be unusually high or low. Such deviations can, however, be corrected by taking averages of good and bad years.

Valuations based on current market prices may deviate from those based on cost:

1. For particular assets and groups of similar assets for the same reasons as in 1 and 2 above, though the market may take account of prospects as well as actual earnings. However, the same principle of cancellation will apply.
2. In particular years for reason 3 above.
3. Because the yield on which market valuations are based fluctuates around the normal level. In this connexion it may be noted that quite large fluctuations in equity markets can take place, as in 1957, without any significant change in earnings. Where there is a significant change in earnings, however, fluctuations in prices have tended in recent years to be greater than variations in earnings, whereas one would expect the market to have an eye on future prospects and to take comparatively little account of fluctuations in earnings that appear to be purely temporary. This phenomenon might be explained either in terms of a kind of 'myopia' affecting markets or by other factors, such as monetary policy, causing fluctuations in the yield basis which the market considers appropriate. In any case, the effect of these fluctuations can be ironed out by taking an average of good and bad years.
4. Because of exogenous influences either affecting particular assets (such as the dividend policy of a particular firm) or general such as dividend limitation or rent restriction.

To sum up, provided that there are no artificial controls on the return to particular types of asset, and that estimates are based on an average of several valuations covering good and bad years, there will be a tendency for the total value of capital measured by capitalization of income to approximate both to the total reached by direct valuation at market price and to that compiled on the basis of cost. There may, however, be marked divergencies in the case of individual assets or industrial groups and in the totals at single dates.

If we now drop the assumption of constant prices, we have again to distinguish between original and replacement cost. If prices are rising, replacement cost will, of course, exceed original cost and, at the end of a long period of inflation, the difference may be substantial.

If we can assume that the idea of a normal yield is still valid, the condition for an increase in the stock of any kind of asset is that its return on replacement cost should be more than normal, and the relationships allowed above between market value, capitalized income, and cost now hold for replacement cost.

The problems of valuing financial assets are basically the same as those of real assets in that the ideal valuation should be meaningful to the holder and consistent both from the point of view of balance-sheet consolidation and integration with a flow of funds analysis.

The main methods of valuation are nominal value, market value, book value, and surrender value.

Most financial claims have a nominal value at which they stand in the accounts of the person or institution of which they are a liability. Shares of no par value and annuities are about the only exceptions, and in the case of annuities the institution owning them normally shows their capital value in its accounts. The significance of nominal values differs very widely from one asset to another. In the case of bank deposits and similar claims possessing almost perfect liquidity, it is the only value that has any economic meaning. In the case of non-marketable debts, such as a personal IOU, it is the only value that it is possible to use. For redeemable obligations near to maturity nominal value will approximate very closely to market value, but for irredeemable fixed interest obligations it has very little meaning, except in conjunction with the 'coupon' rate of interest. By itself it is at best only a record of what has been paid in the past for the right to a fixed annual payment, and it need not even be that, for the obligation may originally have been sold at either above or below 'par'. Finally, for ordinary shares, the nominal value merely tells us the minimum amount that has been paid in the past,[1] by the original shareholders or, in the case of bonus issues, transferred from the reserves of the company. In itself, the nominal value of ordinary shares bears no relation to any other measure of value, though ordinary shares and free reserves together indicate the balance-sheet value of assets 'belonging' to equity holders.

Market value is, of course, the most meaningful concept of value to the holder of an asset and, in calculations of the net worth of any particular sector, its financial assets should be taken at market value. In the case of ordinary shares, market value also provides an indication of the value of the real assets 'belonging' to equity holders. The relationship of this to other measures of the value of real assets has been discussed above. Statistics based on market values have, however, the big disadvantage that, since prices are subject to considerable fluctuation, they give no indication of net purchases or sales of any asset, and cannot be incorporated into a flow of funds analysis. Market values bear no close relationship to the nominal values in which financial claims stand in the balance-sheets of the institutions to which they are a liability, and cannot therefore be used without adjustment in a system of consolidated balance-sheets. Finally, even the institutions who hold them as an asset quite often record them in their balance-sheet at something other than market value.

The basis on which financial claims are valued as assets in the books of their holders has little logic about it and varies very widely between different institutions. The basic criterion is usually cost at time of acquisition, and some institutions, including a great many charities, show only this. Some charities, most non-financial companies, and some financial institutions including the clearing banks give the total market value of investments in a note to the balance-sheet but without giving a figure for any particular class of asset. Others, including most non-banking financial institutions, give book values without any

[1] Companies are not allowed by law to issue ordinary shares at less than their nominal value, though they may and often do issue them at a premium.

mention of market values. It appears that institutions following this practice frequently write down their book values if the market value falls and occasionally, though much less frequently, write them up when the market price rises. On the whole, therefore, this practice probably leads to an understatement of market values and to the accumulation of hidden reserves. A few institutions provide complete investment schedules showing both nominal and market values for each item, but they are a very small minority.

Finally, there is a group of assets which are not marketable but which can be converted into cash at a surrender value. The two most important are life assurance policies and pension rights in some schemes. To be strictly logical one should probably use surrender values for these assets in contexts where it would be proper to use market value for marketable securities. On the other hand, surrender values have little economic significance. They are generally below the actuarial present value of the prospective benefit and well below the value of the assets accumulated by the insurance company or pension fund against its liabilities, and the proportion of assets[1] which are in fact surrendered is comparatively small.

For our present study we have divided the economy into nine main sectors, and a number of sub-sectors. The main sectors are: the central government, including the Bank of England and the savings banks; local authorities; public corporations; persons; non-financial companies operating mainly within Great Britain; the banking system, including the merchant banks and the discount houses; non-banking financial institutions; charities and similar non-profit-making organizations; and the world overseas, including British companies operating mainly abroad. Each of these is the subject of a separate chapter, giving its precise definition, a brief account of the sources of information and methods of processing, and comment on the reliability of the results.

[1] There are a considerable number of surrenders among industrial life policies and in pension schemes for weekly paid workers, but the accounts involved are usually very small.

The sources of information naturally varied a good deal between different sectors, but they were of four main kinds. For persons the estate duty statistics were the main source. For government, nationalized industry, public companies, and most financial institutions the basic sources were published accounts and balance-sheets. For pension funds and certain types of charity a special inquiry was made by questionnaire. Finally, there is a section of the field for which little information is available from any of these sources and where references have to be drawn from widely scattered and often flimsy evidence; the most important of these are the Bank of England and the Exchange Equalization Account; private companies; and large parts of the overseas sector.

Our methods of valuation have been determined partly by the theoretical considerations outlined above and partly by the nature of the source material. In the chapters dealing with individual sectors the information is presented on the method of valuation used in the source. In the integrated tables of Chapter 12 adjustments are made in order to achieve some measure of consistency, though complete consistency was not possible. Real assets are taken at balance-sheet value except for persons, where the estate duty statistics dictate a market value basis, and a few charities, including most Oxford and Cambridge colleges, where estimates had to be made by capitalizing income. Cash and bank deposits, trade and other debts, mortgages, bills of exchange, and all fixed interest securities are taken at their nominal values, and ordinary shares at their market value. Finally, life assurance policies and pension rights are entered at the value of the funds held against them by the institutions concerned.

This requires a number of adjustments to our original figures, and these are given in detail in the notes to Chapter 12. Each column of the integrated tables shows the assets of the sector or sub-sector concerned, and each asset is entered at its adjusted value, the sum of the adjustments is then entered, with sign reversed at the foot of the column, so that the total is brought back to that of the balance-sheet or other basic source of information. In the same way, each row shows the liabilities of a sector or sub-sector and, when these are entered at a value different from that of the balance-sheet, a compensating item is included in the adjustment column at the right of the tables. In most cases these adjustments are not so large as might have been expected. The tables are not, of course, consolidated balance-sheets, but contain the ingredients from which these could be constructed and it is fairly easy to select from them the items relevant to each of the concepts of national wealth discussed at the beginning of the chapter. This is done in Chapter 12.

2

THE CENTRAL GOVERNMENT

DEFINITION OF THE SECTOR

OUR definition, with three exceptions mentioned later, coincides with that of the National Income Blue Book. This is described as comprising, 'All bodies for whose estimates a Minister of the Crown or other responsible person is accountable to Parliament. One of the marks of such accountability is that such bodies submit to Parliament detailed statements of their estimated and actual expenditure and their collection of revenue.'[1]

The main components of the sector are:

1. The civil, revenue, and defence departments, whose activities are classified as 'supply services'.
2. Non-departmental organizations whose expenditure is subject to departmental control, including the regional hospital boards and the Atomic Energy Authority. A full list is given in *National Income Statistics, Sources and Methods*, p. 225.
3. The 'Extra-Budgetary Funds'. The most important are the National Insurance Funds, the Post Office and Trustee savings banks, the Exchange Account, and the Bank of England. There are, however, a large number of smaller funds, not all of which publish accounts. Only the ordinary business of the Trustee savings banks is included here; their Special Investment Departments are treated as financial institutions and included in Chapter 9.

The three differences between our classification and that of the Blue Book are:

1. We exclude Northern Ireland.

[1] *National Income Statistics, Sources and Methods*, p. 179, London, H.M.S.O., 1956. Hereafter referred to as *Sources & Methods*.

2. We include both the Issue and Banking Departments of the Bank of England in extra-budgetary funds, whereas the Blue Book includes only the Issue Department, and treats the Banking Department as a Public Corporation.
3. The Metropolitan Police are treated as part of the central government in the Blue Book even though their financial statistics are published with those of local authorities. We treat them as a local authority and include them in Chapter 4.

THE ASSETS OF THE CENTRAL GOVERNMENT

The assets of the central government can be divided into three broad categories.

First, there is an important group of real assets representing the capital employed by the government in one or other of its direct economic activities. Among these real assets are the buildings, plant, equipment, and stocks of trading departments; the buildings owned and occupied by the government for administrative purposes; and temporary houses built by direct government finance after the Second World War. The dividing line between the central government and other branches of the public sector is sometimes rather an arbitrary one. For example, the Post Office and the Atomic Energy Authority are treated as part of the central government, but it is purely an accident of history that neither was made a public corporation. Again, temporary houses are treated as 'belonging' to the central government because they were directly financed by it, whereas permanent houses financed by local authorities out of loans from the Public Works Loans Board are treated as 'belonging' to local authorities. These anomalies are inevitable, but many of them disappear in our consolidated balance-sheet of the public sector in Chapter 5.

Secondly, the government owns financial assets which are liabilities of some other sector. These include advances to public corporations and local authorities; shares in a few companies, such as the Suez Canal Co., and the British Petroleum Co.;

loans to foreign governments and the reserves of the Exchange Equalization Account.

Thirdly, there are holdings by the government of its own securities, mainly in the various 'extra-budgetary funds'. The logical way of treating these in a consolidated balance-sheet is to omit them altogether and to make a corresponding deduction from the national debt on the other side of the account. Where the holding of securities is purely an internal accounting matter, e.g. in the case of the Treasury bill holding of the Exchange Account, this is quite simple. In other cases, however, the government securities are the counterpart of liabilities to another sector, e.g. deposits in the Post Office Savings Bank. In such cases, the liability should, of course, be shown, and this problem is discussed further in connexion with the liabilities side of the balance-sheet.

REAL ASSETS

Table 1 summarizes the assets of the Post Office and those government agencies whose balance-sheets appear in the annual *Trading Accounts and Balance Sheets*. Together, they had fixed assets valued at over £500 m. in 1953 and more than £600 m. in 1955. By far the most important of these organizations was the Post Office, whose fixed assets were valued at £374 m. in 1953 and £461 m. in 1955. The Royal Ordnance factories and the Board of Trade factories in development areas are the only other large items. At the other end of the scale the State Management Districts own public houses in Carlisle and Gretna valued at just under £1 m.

Stocks and work in progress amounted to £459 m. in 1953 and £244 m. in 1955, a decline that reflected the gradual winding-up of the government commodity trading schemes introduced during the Second World War. The main holders of stocks were, of course, the Ministry of Materials (subsequently the Commodity Trading Division of the Board of Trade) and the Ministry of Food. The holdings of these two ministries fell from £347 m. in 1953 to £114 m. in 1955.

There are several other activities of the central government not covered by the agencies in Table 1. The Atomic Energy

TABLE 1

Assets of government trading agencies[1]

£ m. at 31 March

	1953	*1954*	*1955*
1. Land and buildings	165	173	185
2. Plant and equipment	341	382	416
3. Total fixed assets	506	555	601
4. Stocks	459	410	244
5. Debtors:			
(*a*) British government	191	203	215
(*b*) Foreign government	1	1	..
(*c*) Other	118	105	65
6. Investments	5	5	6
7. Cash:			
(*a*) With Paymaster-General	5	4	11
(*b*) Other	20	15	10
Total	1,305	1,299	1,152

Authority presented its first account for the year ending on 31 March 1955, when its balance-sheet showed the following figures:

	£ *m.*
Land and buildings	48
Plant and machinery	85
Stocks and work in progress	25
Total	158

The *Civil Appropriation Accounts* show grants for capital purposes to the Authority and its predecessor the Atomic Energy

[1] Departments included are the Ministry of Food, the Board of Trade (Commodity Trading and Development Areas), the Post Office, Royal Ordnance Factories, the Mint, the Forestry Commission, County Agricultural Executive Committee, the State Management Districts, and the Stationery Office. Sources: *Post Office Commercial Accounts* and *Trading Accounts and Balance Sheets*, H.M.S.O. Annual.

Department of £21·9 m. in 1954–5 and £5·5 m. in 1953–4. On the other hand, the Authority showed depreciation of £11 m. for the period from 1 August 1954 to 31 March 1955.

The Crown Lands Commissioners do not publish a balance-sheet but their income account shows an income from rents and royalties which varied between £2·2 m. and £2·4 m., of which about £1 m. was left, after expenses, to be handed over to the Exchequer. It would, therefore, seem reasonable to value the assets of the Commissioners at around £25 m.

Finally, there are temporary houses and schools, married quarters for the Armed Forces and government offices for which we have to rely on the imputed net rent included in the National Income estimates,[1] and plant and machinery rented to private firms by the Ministry of Supply. Taking a value of five years net rent for temporary houses and schools (which were already nearing the end of their allotted life); ten years for plant and machinery and twenty years for permanent houses and offices would give the following capital values:

	£ m.
Temporary houses and schools	130
Plant and machinery .	90
Other houses and offices .	100
Total	320

Summarizing all this information on the real assets of the government (with brackets denoting estimates) we have:

£ m. at 31 March

	1953	*1954*	*1955*
Agencies covered in Table 1 .	965	965	845
Atomic Energy Authority .	(145)	(150)	158
Other government property .	(320)	(320)	(320)
Total	1,430	1,435	1,323

Of this fixed capital, buildings, plant, and machinery accounted for about £950 m. in 1953 and £1,050 m. in 1955.

There are two important omissions from this calculation—the

[1] *Sources and Methods*, p. 196.

value of roads financed by the central government and that of military installations. There is, however, no possible way of setting even an approximate value on these.

FINANCIAL ASSETS

Table 2 shows the financial assets of the central government, analysed according to the sector of which they are liabilities, derived from the Finance Accounts. The Finance Accounts, however, do not cover by any means the whole of the central government as here defined. They exclude the Post Office and Trustee savings banks, the National Insurance Funds, and a number of other departmental funds, while the Bank of England and the Exchange Account are entered at a nominal figure which bears no relation to their actual assets.

This raises the whole vexed question of the holdings of the group of official agencies usually known as 'the Departments'. The available information is very incomplete and the government has consistently refused to add to it. The savings banks, the National Insurance Funds, and a number of smaller funds publish annual accounts including a schedule of their security holdings, but the value of this is limited by the fact that accounts relate to different dates—those of the Trustee savings banks to 20 November, the Post Office Savings Bank to 31 December, and the National Insurance Funds to 31 March. Since 1951 the total amount of the national debt held by government departments has been published in a footnote to Part I, Capital Account, of the annual *National Debt Return*,[1] which also distinguishes between the floating debt and 'other national debt'. The note does not list the departments concerned, but it does state

[1] 1953, Cmd. 8975; 1954, Cmd. 9297; 1955, Cmd. 9621.

Footnotes to Table 2, page 23.

[1] Excluding advances to N. Ireland, included in section 5, and investments, included in Table 3.

[2] The entry of B.P. shares at cost and Suez Canal shares at estimated market value follows the practice of the *Finance Accounts*. The B.P. shares would have had a market value of about £80 m. in 1953, £125 m. in 1954, and £210 m. in 1955.

[3] Loans to China are excluded from this item, as they are presumably now worthless.

TABLE 2

Assets of the central government as given in 'Finance Accounts of the United Kingdom'

£m. at 31 March

	1953	*1954*	*1955*
1. Assets which are liabilities of other central government agencies:			
(*a*) Exchange Equalization Account	675	675	975
(*b*) Bank of England capital	58	58	58
(*c*) Under Export Guarantees Act	25	22	23
(*d*) Civil Contingencies Fund	31	21	16
(*e*) Others	8	8	8
	798	783	1,081
2. Liabilities of Public Corporations:			
(*a*) Coal Industry Acts	361	442	543
(*b*) New Towns Acts	48	78	107
(*c*) Cotton. Centralized Buying Act	92	50	25
(*d*) Cinematograph Film Production Act	6	6	6
(*e*) Development of Inventions Act	..	1	1
(*f*) Cable and Wireless	30	30	30
(*g*) Colonial Development Corporation	30	36	40
(*h*) Overseas Food Corporation	4	4	..
(*i*) Housing (Scotland) Act, 1950	38	47	53
	609	694	805
3. Liabilities of Local Authorities:			
(*a*) Land settlement loans outstanding	10	10	10
(*b*) Building Materials and Housing Act, 1945	2	2	..
(*c*) Local loans fund and redemption of local loans[1]	2,262	2,536	2,865
	2,275	2,548	2,875
4. Liabilities of British Companies:			
(*a*) British Sugar Corporation	1	1	1
5. Liabilities of external sector:			
(*a*) British Petroleum Co. (shares at cost)[2]	5	5	5
(*b*) Suez Canal shares (estimated market value)	27	27	36
(*c*) Advances to allied governments	246	201	189
(*d*) Advances to Germany and Austria[3]	1	147	142
(*e*) Advances to colonies	11	16	32
(*f*) Advances to other governments	39	16	12
	329	412	416
Total	4,012	4,438	5,178

For footnotes see page 22.

that 'These figures do not include the holdings of the Issue Department of the Bank of England and the Exchange Equalization Account, nor holdings of the Public Trustee, the Charity Commissioners, and other similar Trustee Bodies'. These figures are as follows:

£ m. at 31 March

	1953	*1954*	*1955*
Floating debt . . .	321	344	336
Other debt . . .	3,236	3,203	3,220

Table 3 analyses the holdings of published accounts according to the sector of which they are a liability. The accounts included in the table are those of the Post Office Savings Bank, the Trustee

TABLE 3

Financial assets in published departmental accounts

£ m.
Accounting date nearest to 31 March

	1953	*1954*	*1955*
1. Liabilities of central government:			
(*a*) Floating debt . . .	54	68	61
(*b*) Quoted securities . . .	2,038	2,032	2,019
(*c*) Unquoted securities . .	1,646	1,644	1,612
2. Liabilities of public corporations:			
(*a*) Quoted securities . . .	568	534	623
(*b*) Unquoted securities . .	97	106	105
3. Liabilities of local authorities .	5	5	4
4. Liabilities of external sector .	3	1	1
5. Interest accrued . . .	20	20	19
6. Cash and other assets . .	2	4	2
Total	4,432	4,413	4,446

savings banks, the National Insurance Fund, the County Court Fund, the Irish Land Purchase Fund, the Crown Lands Commissioners, the Death Duties Surrendered Securities Fund, the Local Loans Fund, and the National Land Fund. Altogether these funds held assets of over £4,400 m. of which the Post Office Savings Bank accounted for over £1,700 m., the Trustee savings banks over £800 m., and the National Insurance Fund £1,600 m. Of these vast sums all but a trivial amount was in government securities or the securities of nationalized industries. More than £2,500 m. was in securities quoted on the Stock Exchange and the balance in the floating debt or in various forms of unquoted security, chiefly special annuities issued to the Post Office and Trustee savings banks.

There are certain discrepancies between the figures given in the *National Debt Return* and those of Table 3. The table includes Victory Bonds and Funding Loan surrendered in payment of death duties and held by the National Debt Commissioners, also various items classified as 'Other Capital Liabilities', both of which are excluded from the figure given in the National Debt Return. Further, the value of annuities held by the savings banks is taken at their accounting dates in our tables and at 31 March in the National Debt Return. Adjustment for these items gives the following result:

Government securities other than floating debt

£m.

	1953	*1954*	*1955*
From Table 3	3,684	3,676	3,631
less			
Bonds surrendered for death duties	−91	−88	−86
'Other capital liabilities'	−257	−298	−310
Adjustment for annuities	−12	−12	−13
Total	3,324	3,278	3,229
Compared with National Debt Return	3,236	3,203	3,220

These discrepancies could be largely explained by differences in accounting dates, and it appears that the unpublished accounts held only small amounts of non-floating debt.

The position in respect of the floating debt is very different. Here the comparison is as follows:

£m. at 31 March

	1953	*1954*	*1955*
National Debt Return	321	344	336
Published accounts	54	68	61
Differences	267	276	275

Clearly a large part of departmental holdings of the floating debt is in unpublished accounts.

Any estimate of the holdings of the Exchange Account is bound to be subject to a very wide margin of error. Mr. D. S. Lees has estimated the Treasury bill holding of the Account by the process of taking its capital less the cumulative total of its net gold purchases (at estimated cost) since it began operations.[1] His calculations give an estimated bill holding at March 1938 of £165 m. Continuation of this process for the war and post-war years involves making allowances for changes in the valuation of gold, for changes in the Account's holdings of non-dollar currencies (about which information is available only intermittently), and for the Account's purchases of dollar securities during the war (about which there is no official information at all). Even if it were possible to make all these adjustments exactly, the method of calculation would underestimate the resources of the Account because it ignores its normal working profit. The essence of the Account's operations is that it buys gold or dollars when they are cheap in terms of sterling and sells when they are dear. The margin is small, but the volume of transactions is very large, and the cumulative profits over nearly twenty years must have been substantial. My very tentative estimate is that the Account held approximately £250 m. of bills at the end of March 1953, £70 m. at the corresponding date in 1954, and £370 m. in 1955.

The decline in the bill holding between 1953 and 1954 is the result of a gain of £185 m. in reserves, while the capital of the Account remained constant, and the increase from 1954 to 1955 is the result of a £300 m. increase in the capital of the Account, while the reserves remained practically constant. These figures are rather lower than some other estimates, but they gain some support from the timing of the increase in the Account's capital in 1954. The reserves rose by £48 m. in April and £59 m. in May, and the increase in the Account's capital occurred during the second week in May.

[1] D. S. Lees, 'Public Departments and Cheap Money', *Economica*, Feb. 1955, p. 79.

The Exchange Account also holds a substantial amount of dollar securities. During the war the government bought dollar securities from private citizens and borrowed others; many of these securities were deposited with the Reconstruction Finance Corporation as collateral for a loan of $425 m. The loan was eventually repaid, partly out of investment income, and partly by sales, and the British government recovered possession of the remaining collateral in 1951. Nothing has been disclosed either of the amount of the securities initially deposited, the amount sold in America to repay the capital of the R.F.C. loan, or the amount of borrowed securities returned to their owners. It was, therefore, impossible to form any idea of the value of securities remaining in the Exchange Account until the time of the Suez crisis, when it was stated in Parliament that their value was between $750 m. and $1,000 m.[1] It is also known that the securities were mainly industrials, and that sales of about $30 m. were made in 1955. The Securities and Exchange Commission Index of Industrial Stocks, which averaged 345 for 1956, was 193 in 1953, 230 in 1954, and 305 in 1955. It seems reasonable, therefore, to put the sterling value of these securities at around £180 m. in 1953; £220 m. in 1954, and £280 m. in 1955.

Table 4 shows the consolidated account of the Bank of England Issue and Banking Departments. Notes held in the Banking Department (the balance between the legal fiduciary issue and the notes actually in circulation) appear in the Bank Return as a liability of the Issue Department and an asset of the Banking Department. They, therefore, disappear on consolidation. The other items are arranged according to the sectors of which they are a liability. The item 'Other Securities' in the Bank Return is subdivided into 'Discounts and Advances' and 'Securities'. The tradition is that the former represents assets acquired by the Bank on the initiative of the market, and the latter, assets acquired on the Bank's own initiative. The normal way for the market to borrow in recent years has been by taking seven-day loans against Treasury bills. Hence we have treated 'discounts and advances' as a government liability and 'securities' as a

[1] *The Economist*, 8 Dec. 1956, contains a report of the statement.

liability of the private sector. Coin, other than gold, is regarded as a government liability, and gold as a liability of the external sector.

TABLE 4

Bank of England Consolidated account of the issue and banking departments

£ m.

	1 April 1953	*31 March 1954*	*30 March 1955*
Liabilities:			
1. To central government:			
(*a*) Capital and rest	19	19	19
(*b*) Public deposits	46	32	16
2. To other sectors:			
(*a*) Notes in circulation	1,509	1,577	1,696
(*b*) Bankers' deposits	269	263	276
(*c*) Other deposits	75	73	66
Total	1,918	1,963	2,072
Assets:			
3. Liabilities of central government:			
(*a*) Government debt	11	11	11
(*b*) Government securities	1,878	1,914	2,023
(*c*) 'Discounts and Advances'	10	15	16
(*d*) Coin other than gold	2	2	2
4. Liabilities of other sectors:			
(*a*) 'Securities'	14	17	16
(*b*) Gold coin and bullion	3	3	3
Total	1,918	1,963	2,072

The type of security held by both the Bank and the Exchange Account is a closely guarded secret; it is believed, however, that the sterling assets of the Exchange Account are held in 'tap' Treasury bills and that the Bank holds both Treasury bills and a large portfolio of quoted government securities. Comparison of the figures given above with those for the floating debt gives a faint clue to the order of magnitude of these holdings.

During the period with which we are concerned, it can be assumed that all 'tap' Treasury bills and all Ways and Means

Advances were in the hands of government agencies.[1] The relevant figures may, therefore, be summarized as follows:

£m. at 31 March

	1953	*1954*	*1955*
Floating debt held by departments covered by National Debt Return . . .	321	344	336
Estimated sterling assets of Exchange Account . .	250	70	370
Government securities held by Bank of England . .	1,878	1,914	2,023
	2,449	2,328	2,729
Tap bills and Ways and Means Advances . . .	1,850	1,699	2,057
Difference. . . .	599	629	672

Assuming that the Exchange Account does not hold any significant amount of securities other than bills or Ways and Means, the difference shown at the foot of the table gives the minimum Bank of England holding of quoted government securities, and 'tender' bills. The true holding would be higher by the amount, if any, of our underestimate of the sterling assets of the Exchange Account, and the amount of the 'hidden reserve' of the Bank of England.

A final item in the assets of the state, about which information is available, is the amount of income tax, surtax, and profits taxes due. The figures of taxation outstanding in the Inland Revenue Reports refer only to arrears, and take no account of current tax liabilities. We have, therefore, taken the figures for public corporations and companies from the balance-sheets of Chapters 3 and 7. For persons, we have been obliged to use the Inland Revenue figures, and we have assumed that persons are responsible for a quarter of outstanding income-tax, and the whole of surtax and 'special contribution'. This, however, understates personal liabilities since it is not possible to allow for current surtax and current personal liabilities under schedule D assessments.

[1] The practice of issuing 'tap' bills to Dominion and Colonial holders of sterling balances ceased after 1951. E. Nevin, *The Problem of the National Debt*, University of Wales Press Board, Cardiff, 1954, p. 39.

Table 5 brings together the available information about the real assets of the central government, and about those financial

TABLE 5

Assets of the central government according to sector of liability

£m. at 31 March

	1953	*1954*	*1955*
Real assets:			
1. Fixed capital	950	1,000	1,050
2. Stocks	480	435	273
	1,430	1,435	1,323
Financial assets:			
3. Liabilities of public corporations:			
(*a*) Exchequer (Table 2)	609	694	805
(*b*) Other departments (Table 3)	665	640	728
(*c*) Taxation due	52	70	59
	1,326	1,404	1,592
4. Liabilities of local authorities:			
(*a*) Exchequer (Table 2)	2,275	2,548	2,875
(*b*) Other departments (Table 3)	5	5	4
	2,280	2,553	2,879
5. Liabilities of domestic private sector:			
(*a*) Shares held by government (Table 2)	1	1	1
(*b*) Debts to trading agencies (Table 1)	118	105	65
(*c*) Bank of England 'securities' (Table 4)	14	17	16
(*d*) Taxation due	1,176	1,155	1,248
	1,309	1,278	1,330
6. Liabilities of external sector:			
(*a*) Exchequer (Table 2)	329	412	416
(*b*) Other departments (Table 3)	3	1	1
(*c*) Debts to trading agencies (Table 1)	1	1	..
(*d*) Exchange Account:			
(i) gold and dollar reserve	774	959	953
(ii) estimated dollar securities	180	220	280
(*e*) Bank of England, gold coin and bullion	3	3	3
	1,290	1,596	1,653
Total	7,635	8,266	8,777

assets which are liabilities of other sectors, and Table 6 summarizes our estimates of the government's holding of its own securities. In compiling this table it is assumed that the figures of public holdings of the national debt given in the National Debt Return include all the accounts in section I of Table 2 except the Bank of England and the Exchange Account, and all those in Table 3, as well as the unpublished accounts. The only additions to these

TABLE 6

Holdings of the national debt by government agencies

£m. at 31 March

	1953	*1954*	*1955*
1. 'Tap' bills and Ways and Means Advances:			
(*a*) National Debt Return	321	344	336
(*b*) Exchange Account (estimates)	250	70	370
(*c*) Bank of England (estimates)	1,279	1,285	1,351
	1,850	1,699	2,057
2. Other national debt:			
(*a*) National Debt Return	3,236	3,203	3,220
(*b*) 'Other Capital Liabilities' held by departments	257	298	310
(*c*) Funding Loan and Victory Bonds surrendered for death duties	91	88	86
(*d*) Bank of England (estimated)	620	655	699
Total	6,054	5,943	6,372

figures are, therefore, for 'Other Capital Liabilities' and Funding Loan and Victory Bonds surrendered for death duties (p. 23), and our estimate of the holdings of the Bank of England and the Exchange Account.

THE LIABILITIES OF THE CENTRAL GOVERNMENT

The liabilities of the central government consist of:

1. The national debt, including 'other capital liabilities' and post-war credits, less the holdings of government agencies.
2. The deposits in Post Office and Trustee savings banks.
3. The debts of government trading departments.
4. Notes and coin in circulation. This last item may seem rather artificial as there is no real way in which these liabilities can be discharged. However, since their holders obviously treat them as assets, and they are clearly not a

liability of any other sector, it is convenient to include them here. Moreover, there is a further element of logic in so doing, as a decline in the note circulation would reduce the amount of government securities held by the Bank of England, and so force the government to borrow more from some other source.

Contingent liabilities in respect of guaranteed loans are not included, and neither are liabilities in respect of unfunded pension schemes for civil servants or the National Insurance Fund.

The composition of the national debt is shown in Table 7. The

TABLE 7

The composition of the national debt

	31 March 1953		*31 March 1954*		*31 March 1955*	
	£ m.	%	*£ m.*	%	*£ m.*	%
1. Internal:						
(*a*) Floating debt	4,713	17·46	4,819	17·50	5,247	18·83
(*b*) Quoted securities	13,932	51·62	14,520	52·73	14,572	52·28
(*c*) Small Savings securities	2,570	9·52	2,551	9·26	2,620	9·40
(*d*) Other unquoted securities	1,909	7·07	1,876	6·81	1,846	6·62
(*e*) Other capital liabilities	264	0·98	305	1·11	310	1·11
(*f*) Post-war credits	581	2·15	564	2·04	540	1·94
	23,969	88·81	24,635	89·45	25,135	90·18
2. External—payable in sterling:						
(*a*) International financial institutions	758	2·81	693	2·52	510	1·83
(*b*) Other	99	0·37	96	0·35	96	0·34
3. External—payable in foreign currencies:						
(*a*) International financial institutions	..	..	..	..	59	0·21
(*b*) Other	2,163	8·01	2,115	7·68	2,071	7·43
Total	26,989		27,539		27,871	

broad distinction drawn in the *Finance Accounts* between internal and external debt refers to where the debt is payable rather than by whom it is held. All the external debt is held externally, but foreign persons and institutions also hold a considerable amount of the internal debt as will appear in Chapter 11.

Of the internal debt, nearly 60 per cent. consists of securities quoted on the Stock Exchange; the floating debt ('tap' and 'tender' Treasury bills and Ways and Means Advances) accounts for about another 20 per cent., though this amount is subject to a good deal of fluctuation. Small savings securities (savings certificates and defence bonds) account for roughly one-tenth of the internal debt, and the remaining large item, 'other unquoted securities', consists mainly of annuities issued to the savings banks. 'Other Capital Liabilities' comprise borrowings under the Post Office Telegraph Acts and are again largely held by the savings banks. Finally, there is the liability of the state for post-war credits, which are not treated as part of the national debt in the *Finance Accounts*, but which are given in the Inland Revenue Reports.

External debt payable in sterling includes small amounts of loans from the colonies and former colonies, but is mainly the sterling part of the British subscription to the International Monetary Fund and the World Bank, together with the unfunded part of our cumulative deficit with the European Payments Union. The main items among external loans payable in foreign countries are, of course, the dollar loans raised at the end of 1945 from the United States and Canada.

The debts of the government trading agencies shown in Table 1 were:

£m. at 31 March

	1953	*1954*	*1955*
Foreign government . .	2·5	1·4	0·6
Other	97·6	101·8	40·7
Total	100·1	103·2	41·3

Bank of England notes in circulation are shown in Table 4 and the estimated coinage in circulation (shown in the *Monthly Digest of Statistics*) was:

£m. March

1953	*1954*	*1955*
155	159	162

We are now in a position to construct the consolidated statement of the assets and liabilities of the state shown in Table 8. Summing up this table, in round figures, for 1955, the state held about £1,300 m. of real assets, claims on public corporations of nearly £1,600 m., and on local authorities of nearly £2,900 m. representing real assets created by these institutions with funds borrowed from the state. It held financial claims on the domestic private sector of over £1,300 m. including taxation due, and over £1,650 m. of such claims on the external sector. It also held over £6,350 m. of its own securities. On the other hand, it had over £18,750 m. of internal debt owned by other sectors, over £2,700 m. of external debt, and £2,770 m. owing to savings bank depositors, besides its notional liability for the note circulation and coinage. The item of £17,398 m. excess liabilities which would look very odd in any other balance-sheet has, of course, a simple explanation. The borrowing of an ordinary trading organization is for the creation of real assets and, if these assets should fall in value, it is normal practice to write down the value of the liabilities. Most of the borrowing of the central government, however, has been not for the creation of real assets but for the finance of war. Hence, while the true value of an industrial stock or share lies in the claim which it gives upon the earning power of real assets, that of a government bond lies in the claim which it gives on the tax revenue of the government. These securities are, however, assets from the point of view of their owners, and form part of the net worth of the private sector, as defined in Chapter 1, though not of the national wealth.

TABLE 8

Consolidated balance-sheet of the central government at 31 March

£m.

Liabilities	1953	1954	1955	Assets	1953	1954	1955
1. Internal debt outside government agencies	17,915	18,692	18,753	8. Fixed capital and stocks	1,430	1,435	1,323
2. Liabilities to L.A.s for hospitals	19	18	16	9. Financial liabilities of:			
3. External debt	3,020	2,904	2,736	(*a*) Public corporations	1,326	1,404	1,592
4. Debts of government trading agencies	100	103	42	(*b*) Local authorities	2,280	2,553	2,879
5. Savings bank deposits	2,752	2,738	2,770	(*c*) Domestic private sector	1,309	1,278	1,330
6. Bank of England notes in circulation	1,509	1,577	1,696	(*d*) External sector	1,290	1,596	1,653
7. Coin	155	159	162	10. Excess of net liabilities over assets	17,835	17,925	17,398
Total	25,470	26,191	26,175	Total	25,470	26,191	26,175

3

PUBLIC CORPORATIONS

DESCRIPTION OF SECTOR

OUR sector differs in three ways from that of the National Income Blue Book:

(i) As explained in Chapter 2 the Banking Department of the Bank of England, treated as a public corporation in the Blue Book, is included as part of our central government sector.

(ii) Our exclusion of Northern Ireland leads to the omission of the Electricity Board for Northern Ireland, the Northern Ireland Housing Trust, and the Ulster Transport Authority; and

(iii) The National Service Hostels Association and Festival Gardens Ltd. were excluded because we were unable to obtain the relevant information from them. Their figures are, however, very small in relation to those of the major corporations.

The corporations which our figures cover, in order of their balance-sheet totals at the nearest accounting date to 31 March 1955, are as on p. 38. The Raw Cotton Commission is also included for 1953 and 1954; it presented its last report and accounts for the year ending on 31 August 1954.

Most of the corporations are engaged in industry; their assets consist almost wholly of the fixed and circulating capital employed in the business, and their liabilities, of the loans raised either to create new assets or to compensate former holders. This group is, of course, dominated by the four vast corporations set up between 1947 and 1949 to run the nationalized coal, electricity, gas, and transport industries. Balance-sheet summaries of these four are given separately in Tables 9 to 12.

TABLE 9

British Transport Commission
Summary of balance-sheets, 31 December 1952–4

Liabilities	*1952* (£ m.)	*1953*	*1954*	*Assets*	*1952* (£ m.)	*1953*	*1954*
1. Capital liabilities:				4. Fixed assets:			
(*a*) Quoted stock[1]	1,351	1,358	1,441	(*a*) Land and buildings	998	1,006	1,010
(*b*) Unquoted stock	..	..	..	(*b*) Plant and equipment	393	417	445
(*c*) Loans from central government	..	..	..	(*c*) Goodwill, &c.	64	64	31
				(*d*) Trade investments	12	12	12
(*d*) Other capital liabilities[2]	136	136	134	5. Current assets:			
(*e*) Reserves	14	17	21	(*a*) Stocks and work in progress	105	103	95
2. Current liabilities:				(*b*) Trade and other debtors	76	77	80
(*a*) Bank overdrafts and loans	..	..	..	(*c*) Marketable securities	31	34	86
(*b*) Trade and other creditors	65	68	69	(*d*) Tax reserve certificates	..	..	..
(*c*) Interest and dividends due	11	12	12	(*e*) Cash[4]	48	40	46
(*d*) Current taxation	20	28	14	6. Deficiencies	31	27	39
3. Deferred liabilities and provisions[3]	194	169	187	7. Other assets[5]	32	8	33
Total	1,791	1,788	1,877	Total	1,791	1,788	1,877

[1] Including loan of £40 m. from London Electric Transport Finance Corporation Ltd.

[2] Deposits by staff savings banks and pension funds, obligations to local authorities, and consideration for undertakings acquired to be met by issue of stock.

[3] 'Abnormal maintenance', actuarial deficiencies on guaranteed superannuation funds, and 'other provisions'.

[4] Including deposits at short notice and Treasury bills.

[5] Balance receivable on issue of stock, discounts on issue of stock, and Road Haulage Disposal Account.

There are a number of the smaller corporations, however, whose activities are outside the field of British industry. Cable and Wireless Ltd., the Overseas Food Corporation, and the Colonial Development Corporation operate mainly abroad. The Scottish Special Housing Association and the New Towns Corporations are concerned, as their names imply, with housebuilding and ownership, while the Raw Cotton Commission was a

Name	*Financial year ending*	*Balance-sheet total £ m.*
British Transport Commission	31.12.54	1,876
British Electricity Authority	31.3.55	1,328
National Coal Board	31.12.54	684
Gas Council (with area boards)	31.3.55	541
Iron and Steel Holding and Realization Agency	30.9.54	206
North of Scotland Hydro-Electric Board	31.12.54	122
New Towns Corporations	31.3.55	115
British Overseas Airways Corporation	31.3.55	61
Scottish Special Housing Association	31.3.55	59
Cable and Wireless Ltd.	31.3.55	44
Colonial Development Corporation	31.12.54	42
British European Airways Corporation	31.3.55	24
British Broadcasting Corporation	31.3.55	23
National Dock Labour Board	1.1.55	6
National Film Finance Corporation	31.3.55	6
Overseas Food Corporation	31.3.55	3
National Research Development Corporation	30.6.55	1
Independent Television Authority	31.3.55	0·1

purely trading body. Finally, there is a group of corporations whose activities are administrative and financial and which hold very little in the way of real assets; this group comprises the National Dock Labour Board, the National Film Finance Corporation, the National Research Development Corporation, and, by far the most important, the Iron and Steel Holding and Realization Agency.

THE ASSETS OF PUBLIC CORPORATIONS

Table 13 shows a consolidated balance-sheet of the public corporations. For the most part, this can be derived by simply adding the separate balance-sheets, but a few items which involve duplication—such as liabilities of the North of Scotland Hydro-

TABLE 10

British Electricity Authority
Summary of balance-sheets, 31 March 1953–5

Liabilities (£m.)	*1953*	*1954*	*1955*	*Assets* (£m.)	*1953*	*1954*	*1955*
1. Capital liabilities:				4. Fixed assets:			
(*a*) Quoted stock	741	866	966	(*a*) Land and buildings, plant and equipment	840	954	1,095
(*b*) Unquoted stock	..	..	..	(*b*) Goodwill, &c.	..	..	..
(*c*) Loans from central government	..	..	..	(*c*) Trade investments	1	1	1
(*d*) Other capital liabilities[1]	123	111	99	5. Current assets:			
(*e*) Reserves	17	23	42	(*a*) Stocks and work in progress	71	64	60
2. Current liabilities:				(*b*) Trade and other debtors	68	72	88
(*a*) Bank overdrafts and loans	92	74	113	(*c*) Marketable securities	26	27	43
(*b*) Trade and other creditors	77	74	83	(*d*) Tax reserve certificates	..	..	..
(*c*) Interest and dividends due	..	..	..	(*e*) Cash	4	4	2
(*d*) Current taxation	11	19	19	6. Deficiencies	..	..	..
3. Deferred liabilities and provisions	2	4	4	7. Other assets[2]	54	48	36
Total	1,063	1,171	1,325	Total	1,063	1,171	1,325

[1] Obligations to local authorities and mortgages and other loans transferred on nationalization.
[2] Obligations of North of Scotland Hydro-Electric Board and 'Intangible assets'.

Electric Board to the Central Electricity Authority—have been eliminated.

The total assets of the corporations amounted to more than £4,500 m. in 1953, and to more than £5,100 m. in 1955, of which over 85 per cent. were held by the 'big four' whose balance-sheets are summarized in Tables 9 to 12.

Real assets—land and buildings, plant and equipment, and stocks—account for nearly 80 per cent. of the total and for rather more than 80 per cent. if the Iron and Steel Holding and Realization Agency is excluded. Assets created by the corporations' own investment are valued at cost less depreciation. Assets acquired by nationalization are normally taken at the value at which they stood in the books of transferred undertakings less subsequent depreciation. The excess of compensation actually paid over the book value of assets taken over is shown sometimes as 'Goodwill' and sometimes as 'Excess of compensation' in the balance-sheets of the various corporations.

The item 'Trade and other Debtors' includes balances outstanding on hire-purchase and instalment sales by the gas and electricity boards. These amounted to:

		£ *m.*	
	1953	*1954*	*1955*
Gas . .	28	35	42
Electricity .	14	16	27

The corporations hold substantial investments, which are shown in Table 14. Some corporations include in their investments the stock of other public corporations, and these cross holdings should, strictly, disappear from a consolidated balance-sheet. They have not been eliminated here because not all boards show them separately; they do, however, disappear in the further consolidation of accounts for the public sector as a whole in Chapter 5. 'Unspecified quoted securities' in Table 14 are nearly all held by Cable and Wireless Ltd., which describes them as 'British Government and other securities' in its balance-sheet; in view of the practice of other boards, it may be presumed that they are very largely gilt-edged. 'Subsidiaries and Trade Investments' are composed mainly of shares in and loans to steel

TABLE 11

National Coal Board

Summary of balance-sheets, 31 December 1952–4

Liabilities	1952 (£ m.)	1953 (£ m.)	1954 (£ m.)	*Assets*	1952 (£ m.)	1953 (£ m.)	1954 (£ m.)
1. Capital liabilities:				4. Fixed assets:			
(*a*) Quoted stock	..	..	..	(*a*) Land and buildings, plant			
(*b*) Unquoted stock	..	..	..	and equipment	321	397	478
(*c*) Loans from central govern-				(*b*) Goodwill, &c.	..	..	..
ment	342	427	516	(*c*) Trade investments	1	16	31
(*d*) Other capital liabilities	23	22	19	5. Current assets:			
(*e*) Reserves	3	3	3	(*a*) Stocks and work in progress	100	92	91
2. Current liabilities:				(*b*) Trade and other debtors	58	65	65
(*a*) Bank overdrafts and loans	10	10	10	(*c*) Marketable securities	7	11	2
(*b*) Trade and other creditors	58	61	65	(*d*) Tax reserve certificates	2	..	..
(*c*) Interest and dividends due	19	20	17	(*e*) Cash	1	2	1
(*d*) Current taxation	10	14	18	6. Deficiencies	14	14	17
3. Deferred liabilities and provisions	41	38	38	7. Other assets	..	..	..
Total	505	596	684	Total	504	596	684

TABLE 12

The Gas Council and Area Boards
Summary of consolidated balance-sheets, 31 March 1953–5

Liabilities	*1953*	*1954*	*1955*	*Assets*	*1953*	*1954*	*1955*
	£ m.				£ m.		
1. Capital liabilities:				4. Fixed assets:			
(*a*) Quoted stock	304	373	369	(*a*) Land and buildings, plant			
(*b*) Unquoted stock	..	..	..	and equipment	282	313	348
(*c*) Loans from central govern-				(*b*) Goodwill, &c.	14	14	14
ment	..	..	..	(*c*) Trade investments	3	3	3
(*d*) Other capital liabilities	36	33[1]	33	5. Current assets:			
(*e*) Reserves	13	18[2]	21	(*a*) Stocks and work in progress	44	44	42
2. Current liabilities:				(*b*) Trade and other debtors	81	90	105
(*a*) Bank overdrafts and loans	51	18	66	(*c*) Marketable securities	6	5	6
(*b*) Trade and other creditors	30	34	37	(*d*) Tax reserve certificates	..	..	..
(*c*) Interest and dividends due	2	2	2	(*e*) Cash	3	3	4
(*d*) Current taxation	8	7	6	6. Deficiencies	..	..	..
3. Deferred liabilities and pro-				7. Other assets[3]	20	20	20
visions	9	6	6				
Total	453	492	541	Total	453	492	541

[1] Including Central Guarantee Fund.
[2] Compensation to local authorities, mortgages, and other loans transferred on nationalization and deposits.
[3] 'Balance of Compensation' and 'discount on issue of stock'.

companies by the Iron and Steel Holding and Realization Agency, though the National Coal Board, the British Transport Commission, and the Colonial Development Corporation also hold significant amounts.

The remaining items in Table 13 (apart from cash) are placed on the assets side of the account by convention, not because they have any real value, but because they are the counterpart of a liability. Deficiencies on current account met by borrowing amounted to £69 m. in 1953 and £74 m. in 1955. The British Transport Commission, the National Coal Board, and the Colonial Development Corporation were the major contributors. Discounts on the issue of stock accounted for a further £14 m. Two other large items were those headed 'balance of compensation' in the accounts of the area gas boards and 'Balance of consideration' in those of the British Electricity Authority. These, as already mentioned, are purely balancing items representing the difference between the compensation paid and the book value of the assets taken over. A final item, rather different from the rest, is the 'Road Haulage Disposal Account' shown by the Transport Commission for 1955. The Transport Act, 1953, provided for payments to the Commission from the Transport Fund of the capital losses incurred in disposing of road-haulage undertakings together with £1 m. compensation for disturbance. The account shows the estimated amount of these sums, which are an asset of the Commission and a liability of the government.

THE LIABILITIES OF PUBLIC CORPORATIONS

Apart from current liabilities, of a kind which would be normal in any large trading organization, the liabilities of the public corporations are mainly the sums paid for the creation of new capital assets or the acquisition of old ones. These sums have, however, been raised in various ways. The former owners of nationalized coal, transport, electricity, gas, and iron and steel undertakings were compensated by the issue of government guaranteed stock which is, of course, quoted. The gas and

TABLE 13

Public corporations—consolidated balance-sheet summary
Accounting dates nearest to 31 March 1953–5

Liabilities (£ m.)	1953	1954	1955	Assets (£ m.)	1953	1954	1955
1. Capital liabilities:				4. Fixed assets:			
(*a*) Quoted stock	2,645	2,803	2,951	(*a*) Land and buildings, plant and equipment	3,097	3,411	3,756
(*b*) Unquoted stock	136	148	163	(*b*) Goodwill, &c.	81	80	48
(*c*) Loans from central government	549	649	726	(*c*) Trade investments	283	232	220
(*d*) Other capital liabilities	307	299	293	5. Current assets:			
(*e*) Reserves	80	97	134	(*a*) Stocks and work in progress	385	353	300
2. Current liabilities:				(*b*) Trade and other debtors	371	384	416
(*a*) Bank overdrafts and loans	191	134	194	(*c*) Marketable securities	112	107	174
(*b*) Trade and other creditors	302	298	345	(*d*) Tax reserve certificates	2	..	..
(*c*) Interest and dividends due	33	36	33	(*e*) Cash	62	58	58
(*d*) Current taxation	52	70	59	6. Deficiencies	69	65	74
3. Deferred liabilities and provisions	266	227	241	7. Other assets	99	71	92
Total	4,561	4,761	5,139	Total	4,561	4,761	5,139

electricity industries financed their new investment up to 1955 by periodical issues of quoted stock though in the budget of 1956 this method was changed in favour of direct loans from the Exchequer. The two airways corporations and the Scottish Hydro-Electric Board have issued unquoted stock, mainly to the savings banks, and the shares of Cable and Wireless Ltd. are held by the state. The other corporations have financed their investment mainly by loans from the Exchequer through the appropriate government department.

The item 'Other Capital Liabilities' in Table 13 includes liabilities in respect of nationalized services transferred from local authorities, and deposits by staff savings banks and pension funds. Local authorities are still liable to lenders for certain debts incurred by undertakings transferred to them from the public corporations and are, in turn, entitled to recoup interest and principal from them. These liabilities amounted to £138 m. in 1953, £125 m. in 1954, and £112 m. in 1955; their treatment in local authority statistics is discussed in Chapter 4. There are also small liabilities for mortgages and other loans inherited from nationalized undertakings.

The provision of pensions varies between corporations and is complicated by the variety of schemes inherited from nationalized undertakings. Most of the corporations have independent funds, and their assets are dealt with in Chapter 9. The British Transport Commission and some of the area gas boards, however, have funded schemes, the funds of which are used internally. These funds are entered as 'deposits' in the accounts. The railway scheme has a large actuarial deficiency, which is treated as a contingent liability. To be consistent with our treatment of private schemes we have, however, treated only the deposits as an asset of the personal sector.

Finally, Table 15 shows the relationship of public corporations as a whole with other sectors. The figures for government holdings of the stock of the corporations are taken from Chapter 1, Tables 2 and 3. Those for loans are from the balance-sheets. There are some discrepancies between the balance-sheet figures and those of the *Finance Accounts*, due to differences

TABLE 14

Public corporations
combined schedule of investments

£ m.

	Nearest accounting date to 31 March		
	1953	*1954*	*1955*
1. British government and guaranteed securities	78	68	130
2. Other specified securities[1]	1	1	2
3. Unspecified quoted securities	13	11	11
4. Unquoted securities	23	31	32
5. Subsidiaries and trade investments[2]	283	232	220
Total	398	343	395

[1] Including local authority securities, British public companies, foreign government and municipal stocks and overseas industrials, all in very small amounts.

[2] Of which the Iron and Steel Holding and Realization Agency accounted for £252 m. in 1953, £185 m. in 1954, and £151 m. in 1955.

TABLE 15

Financial relationship between public corporations and other sectors
Accounting dates nearest to 31 March 1953–5

£ m.

Liabilities	*1953*	*1954*	*1955*
1. To central government:			
(*a*) Quoted stock[1]	568	534	623
(*b*) Unquoted stock	127	136	135
(*c*) Loans	549	649	726
(*d*) Interest and dividends	12	13	12
(*e*) Taxation	52	70	59
	1,308	1,402	1,555
2. To local authorities	138	125	112
3. To other sectors:			
(*a*) Quoted stock	2,077	2,269	2,328
(*b*) Unquoted stock	9	12	28
(*c*) Other capital liabilities	169	174	181
(*d*) Bank loans	191	134	194
(*e*) Trade creditors	302	298	345
(*f*) Interest and dividends	21	23	21
4. Internal Accounting items:			
(*a*) Reserves	80	97	134
(*b*) Deferred liabilities and provisions	266	227	241
Total	4,561	4,761	5,139

£ m.

Assets	*1953*	*1954*	*1955*
5. Fixed assets:			
(*a*) Mainly in U.K.	3,067	3,381	3,731
(*b*) Mainly abroad	30	30	25
(*c*) Goodwill	81	80	48
6. Stocks and work in progress	385	353	300
	3,563	3,844	4,104
7. Liabilities of central government:			
(*a*) Securities	91	79	141
(*b*) Deposits and T.R.C.	91	10	1
8. Liabilities of local authorities:			
(*a*) Temporary advances	6	9	20
9. Liabilities of domestic private sector:			
(*a*) Subsidiaries and trade investments	273	220	210
(*b*) Cash	62	58	58
(*c*) Investments	4	3	2
(*d*) Debtors	371	384	416
10. Liabilities of overseas sector:			
(*a*) Investments and trade investments	13	19	21
11. Internal Accounting items:			
(*a*) Deficiencies	69	65	74
(*b*) Other assets	99	71	92
Total	4,561	4,761	5,139

[1] Holdings in published departmental accounts (Chapter 2, Table 3, item 2*a*).

of accounting dates, and adjustments for these are made in Chapter 5. Interest and dividends have been apportioned between the government and other sectors in proportion to the capital held by each.

In 1955 the corporations held more than £3,750 m. (nearly 75 per cent. of their total assets) in fixed capital, and a further £300 m. of stocks and work in progress. They also held about £160 m. of securities and loans of the central government and local authorities, and over £200 m. of the securities of companies which are covered in Chapter 7. Apart from cash, trade debtors, and a small amount of miscellaneous investments, the remaining assets are the various conventional items of no real value discussed above; these amounted to £249 m. in 1953 and to £214 m. in 1955.

On the liabilities side, there was nearly £1,500 m. of loans from the central government and stock held by government agencies, nearly 29 per cent. of total liabilities. A further £2,350 m. of stock (46 per cent. of total liabilities) is held by persons and institutions outside the government. The remaining quarter of the corporations' liabilities comprised a number of items, of which the most important were trade credits (6½ per cent.), bank loans and overdrafts (4 per cent.), liabilities to employees' pension and savings funds (4 per cent.), and reserves and provisions (7 per cent.).

4

LOCAL AUTHORITIES

DEFINITION OF SECTOR

WE have taken the term 'local authorities' to include all bodies making returns of income and expenditure under Part XI of the Local Government Act, 1933, in England and Wales, and the Local Government (Scotland) Act, 1947, for Scotland. These bodies include not only local councils, from county and county borough to rural district, but also a number of boards created for special purposes, such as harbour, river, and drainage boards. The sector is described fairly fully in Chapter IX of *Sources and Methods*. The only difference between our coverage and that of the National Income Blue Book is that the latter treats the Metropolitan Police as part of the central government sector despite the fact that they make returns under the Local Government Act.

LOCAL AUTHORITY ASSETS

(*a*) *Real assets*

Local authorities hold some real assets in connexion with all the many services which they render. By far the largest part are land and buildings, though they also hold some plant and equipment, e.g. refuse destruction plant, dust carts, fire engines, and buses.

The problem of valuation of this capital is a difficult one. Many services are not sold, e.g. parks, fire, police, and education; some are sold at less than their full economic cost, notably housing; and even the trading services are operated on different principles from those of an ordinary commercial enterprise. Hence, any attempt to estimate asset values by capitalizing income would be grossly misleading.

It is also very difficult to use balance-sheet values, as we have done for the central government, public corporation, and company sectors. The Abstracts of Accounts published by the local authorities contain balance-sheets, but these are normally presented for a number of accounts separately, and not in a consolidated form. The work of collecting accounts from a sufficiently large number of authorities and of consolidating their balance-sheets was beyond the resources of this inquiry.

There remains, however, another method which corresponds to the treatment of income in the National Income Blue Book. The imputed gross rental income is taken there, as corresponding to annual loan charges, i.e. interest payments, payments into sinking funds, and capital repayments other than out of sinking funds. By analogy with this, we take the capital value of local authority assets as equivalent to the net loan debt standing against them, i.e. gross loan debt less sinking funds. If provision for amortization was made over the lifetime of the asset, this would be equivalent to valuation at cost less depreciation, which is the normal method of valuation in the balance-sheets of other sectors. In so far as amortization takes place more quickly than the wearing out of the physical asset, this method results, of course, in undervaluation. It also results in undervaluation in that it does not allow for rising prices. In an age of inflation this error may be substantial but it is one which also arises in the use of balance-sheet statistics. It seems, therefore, that this method, while very simple, gives a basis of valuation fairly closely comparable with that used for other sectors; an alternative method of valuation for local authority houses is, however, given in the appendix to this chapter.

Net debt analysed by principal classes of service is given in Table 16. Debt under the heading 'Small Dwellings Acquisition' is not included in this table; this item represents sums borrowed and re-lent to buyers of houses under the Small Dwellings Acquisition Act and other housing acts, and it is, therefore, treated as a financial asset. It will be seen that housing accounted for about 70 per cent. of the value of local authorities' real assets, schools for about 8 per cent., and water installations for a further 6 per cent.

TABLE 16

Local authorities—net loan debt

£ *m. at 31 March*

	1953	*1954*	*1955*
1. Rate fund services:			
(*a*) Housing	2,289·9	2,645·5	2,957·2
(*b*) Education	263·3	309·8	360·9
(*c*) Public Health	132·4	146·3	160·9
(*d*) Highways and Lighting	60·0	62·8	66·3
(*e*) Police	22·4	28·1	33·9
(*f*) Other[1]	135·4	150·1	166·3
Total (1)	2,903·4	3,342·6	3,745·5
2. Trading services:			
(*a*) Water	219·7	236·6	252·5
(*b*) Passenger transport	32·8	33·9	32·9
(*c*) Harbours, Docks, and Piers	108·6	109·2	109·1
(*d*) Other	28·9	29·1	31·2
Total (2)	390·0	408·6	425·6
Grand total (1 and 2)	3,293·4	3,751·3	4,171·1

[1] Excluding loans under the Small Dwellings Acquisition Acts, amounting to:

	1953	*1954*	*1955*
£ *m.*	75·7	95·5	130·9

Sources: *Local Government Financial Statistics* and *Local Financial Returns* (*Scotland*).

(*b*) *Financial assets*

Besides the housing loans referred to in the last paragraph, local authorities hold financial assets in pension funds, sinking funds, and various 'special funds', including some charitable and trust funds. The total sums held in such funds are given in *Local Government Financial Statistics* and *Local Financial Returns, Scotland*, and are summarized in Table 17.

There is no official information concerning the way in which these funds are held, but a research committee of the Institute of Municipal Treasurers and Accountants made a study of local authority investments in 1955, and the results of this have been made available to me through the kindness of the Chairman of the Committee, Mr. T. Watson. The inquiry covered a sample of 88 authorities in England and Wales including the London

County Council; 19 out of 61 counties; 23 out of 83 county boroughs; and 24 out of 319 non-county boroughs. The coverage of the smaller authorities is much thinner, but their funds

TABLE 17

'Special funds' of local authorities

£ m. at 31 March

	1953	*1954*	*1955*
1. Superannuation funds:			
(*a*) England and Wales	260·2	282·9	307·4
(*b*) Scotland	29·6	31·0	32·3
Total	289·8	313·9	339·7
2. Other funds:			
(*a*) England and Wales	127·8	138·5	136·8
(*b*) Scotland	17·0	18·2	18·9
Total	144·8	156·7	155·7
3. All funds:			
(*a*) England and Wales	388·0	421·4	444·2
(*b*) Scotland	46·6	49·2	51·2
Total	434·6	470·6	495·4

are, of course, less important. We have assumed the sample to be representative both for England and Wales and for Scotland, and have distributed the totals of Table 17 between different types of security in the proportions in which they were held by the sample. The result is shown in Table 18 and the total assets of local authorities in Table 19.

LIABILITIES

The following statistical sources have been used:

(i) *Local Government Financial Statistics* and *Local Financial Returns, Scotland*, which give gross debt, sinking funds, and net debt by type of service, but which do not give any information about the type of debt. These figures are summarized in Table 20.

(ii) The *Return of Outstanding Debt* (*England and Wales*), compiled at two-yearly intervals by the Institute of Municipal

TABLE 18

Estimated investments of local authorities

	Percentage in sample	*Estimated totals, £ m. at 31 March*		
	%	*1953*	*1954*	*1955*
1. General funds:				
(*a*) Government securities	34·8	49·8	54·5	54·2
(*b*) Local Authority and Public Boards	11·6	16·6	18·2	18·1
(*c*) Other securities	7·3	10·5	11·4	11·4
(*d*) Uninvested	10·4	14·9	16·3	16·2
(*e*) Used internally	35·9	51·4	56·3	55·9
		143·2	156·7	155·7
2. Superannuation funds:				
(*a*) Government securities	35·1	101·8	110·1	119·3
(*b*) Local Authority and Public Boards	11·1	32·2	34·8	37·7
(*c*) Other securities	8·6	24·9	27·0	29·2
(*d*) Uninvested	1·4	4·1	4·4	4·8
(*e*) Used internally	43·8	127·0	137·4	148·8
		290·0	313·8	339·7
3. All funds:				
(*a*) Government securities	35·0	151·6	164·6	173·5
(*b*) Local Authority and Public Boards	11·3	48·8	53·0	55·8
(*c*) Other securities	8·2	35·4	38·4	40·6
(*d*) Uninvested (cash)	4·4	19·0	20·7	21·0
(*e*) Used internally	41·2	178·4	193·7	204·7
		433·1	470·5	495·2

Special fund balances—from *Local Government Financial Statistics* and *Local Financial Returns* (*Scotland*)—distributed in same proportions as in sample compiled by the I.M.T.A. research committee.

Treasurers and Accountants, and which has been made available to me by the courtesy of the Institute. This return classifies debt according to type of borrowing for London (City, County, and Metropolitan Boroughs), counties and county boroughs, and a sample (about 200 of each) of non-county boroughs and urban districts. The return does not cover rural districts, boards, or miscellaneous authorities. The relevant figures are summarized in Table 21.

The I.M.T.A. figures are larger than those of Table 16 where

TABLE 19. *Estimated assets of local authorities*

£ m. at 31 March

	1953	*1954*	*1955*
1. Real assets:			
Land and building, plant, equipment and stocks	3,293·4	3,751·3	4,171·1
2. Financial assets:			
(*a*) Loans under Small Dwellings Acquisition and other Housing Acts .	75·7	95·6	130·9
(*b*) Government securities . . .	151·6	164·6	173·5
(*c*) Local Authority and Public Boards	48·8	53·0	55·8
(*d*) Other securities	35·4	38·4	40·6
(*e*) Uninvested	19·0	20·7	21·0
(*f*) Used internally	178·4	193·7	204·7
Total financial assets . . .	508·8	566·1	626·1
Total assets	3,802·2	4,317·4	4,797·2

the definitions are comparable. This is because *Local Government Financial Statistics* and *Local Financial Returns, Scotland* exclude residual items of debt in respect of the nationalized services and unapplied balances in consolidated loans funds and loans pools, both of which are included by the I.M.T.A. These amounts were (for all authorities):

£ m. at 31 March

	1953	*1954*	*1955*
Nationalized services	161·7	148·7	131·7
Unapplied balances .	26·8	16·8	16·1

(iii) The Annual Reports of the Public Works Loans Board, which give the amounts of balances outstanding for England and Scotland separately, together with the Acts under which advances were made and their purpose, but with no breakdown by type of authority. The amounts outstanding, excluding advances to nationalized services, were:

	£ m. at 31 March[1]
1953 . .	2,215·4
1954 . .	2,495·5
1955 . .	2,827·9

[1] These figures correspond to the items 'Local Loans Fund' and 'Redemption of Local Loans' in Chapter 1, Table 2. The difference is due to an adjustment for stock issued at a discount.

TABLE 20. *Local authorities—gross loan debt*

£m. at 31 March

	1953	*1954*	*1955*
1. England and Wales:			
(*a*) L.C.C.	180·2	202·8	221·7
(*b*) City of London	14·4	16·9	19·3
(*c*) Metropolitan boroughs	85·3	101·1	118·4
(*d*) County boroughs	946·7	1,075·0	1,183·9
(*e*) County councils	194·2	222·3	255·4
(*f*) Non-county boroughs	483·0	555·7	639·2
(*g*) Urban districts	467·3	538·2	597·2
(*h*) Rural districts	414·5	485·0	547·2
(*i*) Metropolitan Police	2·6	3·4	4·2
(*j*) Metropolitan Water Board	58·8	58·8	58·5
(*k*) Harbour boards	86·3	86·9	87·1
(*l*) Miscellaneous	62·4	68·1	74·5
Total	2,995·7	3,414·2	3,806·4
2. Scotland:			
(*a*) Counties	114·6	132·3	145·6
(*b*) Districts	0·1	0·1	0·1
(*c*) Counties and cities	137·8	157·9	177·5
(*d*) Large burghs	70·1	82·4	93·4
(*e*) Small burghs	73·4	82·8	89·7
(*f*) Joint committees and boards	3·8	4·4	5·2
(*g*) Harbour authorities	14·2	14·8	15·2
Total	414·0	474·7	526·7
3. Transferred liabilities for nationalized services	161·7	148·7	131·7
Great Britain total	3,571·4	4,037·6	4,464·8

Sources: *Local Government Financial Statistics* and *Local Financial Returns (Scotland)*.

(iv) The *Stock Exchange Yearbook*, which gives details of quoted issues, and also an estimate, compiled in the Share and Loan Department, of the nominal and market value of stock outstanding at 31 March of each year. The annual estimates are summarized in Table 22. The only way of breaking down corporation and county stocks by type of authority is by reference to the particulars of the issues. These were, therefore, analysed and the results are shown in Table 23. There are some discrepancies between the totals of Tables 22 and 23, due to the fact that the particulars of issues refer to various dates, whereas the annual valuation is for 31 March.

TABLE 21

Local authorities. Return of outstanding debt, England and Wales

	£ m.	%	£ m.	%	£ m.	%	£ m.	%	£ m.	%
	London City, County, and Boroughs		*Counties and county boroughs*		*Total large authorities*		*Municipal Borough and Urban District*		*Total*	
Sample: *31 March 1952*		All		All		All	211 M.B.	196 U.D.		
Stock	109·3	42·4	257·6	22·7	366·9	26·3	15·4	2·4	382·4	18·7
Public works loans	111·4	43·3	471·3	41·5	582·7	41·8	490·5	74·9	1,073·1	52·4
Mortgages	25·1	9·7	226·0	19·9	251·0	18·0	108·2	16·5	359·3	17·5
Housing bonds and other loans	0·9	0·3	33·4	2·9	34·2	2·5	5·5	0·8	39·7	1·9
Bank overdraft	1·0	0·4	19·0	1·7	20·0	1·4	7·5	1·1	27·5	1·3
Internal advances	9·9	3·8	128·8	11·3	138·7	10·0	27·4	4·2	166·1	8·1
Total gross debt	257·5		1,136·1		1,393·6		654·5		2,048·1	
31 March 1954		All		All		All	209 M.B.	201 U.D.		
Stock	106·5	31·8	264·0	18·5	370·5	21·0	13·8	1·6	384·2	14·7
Public works loans	188·9	56·4	622·9	43·7	811·8	46·1	643·9	74·8	1,455·6	55·5
Mortgages	25·8	7·7	307·2	21·6	333·0	18·9	138·7	16·1	471·6	18·0
Housing bonds and other loans	1·6	0·5	50·7	3·6	52·2	3·0	21·4	2·5	73·6	2·8
Bank overdraft	1·9	0·6	25·6	1·8	27·5	1·6	9·4	1·1	36·9	1·4
Internal advances	10·1	3·0	155·2	10·8	165·3	9·4	33·5	3·9	198·8	7·6
Total gross debt	334·7		1,425·5		1,760·3		860·7		2,620·9	
31 March 1956		All		All		All	214 M.B.	191 U.D.		
Stock	106·5	25·3	270·3	15·8	376·8	17·7	12·2	1·1	389·0	12·2
Public works loans	244·2	58·0	768·4	45·0	1,012·6	47·6	789·9	74·3	1,802·5	56·4
Mortgages	48·0	11·4	394·4	23·1	442·4	20·8	168·0	15·8	610·4	19·1
Housing bonds and other loans	3·4	0·8	72·4	4·2	75·8	3·6	39·0	3·7	114·8	3·6
Bank overdraft	1·9	0·4	34·4	2·0	36·3	1·7	11·8	1·1	48·1	1·5
Internal advances	17·4	4·1	168·2	9·9	185·6	8·7	43·0	4·0	228·6	7·2
Total gross debt	421·4		1,708·1		2,129·5		1,063·9		3,193·4	

Source: *Institute of Municipal Treasurers and Accountants.*

TABLE 22

Nominal and market value of securities of local authorities and public boards, Great Britain and Northern Ireland

£m. at 31 March

	1953		1954		1955	
	Nom.	*Mkt.*	*Nom.*	*Mkt.*	*Nom.*	*Mkt.*
Corporation and county .	410·5	363·6	426·3	394·6	430·8	385·7
Public boards . . .	149·4	121·0	149·0	127·8	148·8	122·4
Total	559·9	484·6	575·3	522·4	579·6	508·1

Source: *Stock Exchange Yearbook.*

TABLE 23

Corporation and county stocks outstanding

£th. Various dates

		1953	1954	1955
England and Wales	Counties . .	26,449	25,982	25,127
	County boroughs .	242,266	239,100	240,967
	Municipal boroughs	13,341	13,310	12,291
	London—County .	101,743	101,743	101,743
	City .	8,202	8,176	8,151
Scotland	Counties . .	12,609	13,512	11,805
	Burghs . . .	13,744	17,464	17,526
Great Britain—Total		418,354	419,287	417,610
Northern Ireland	Belfast . . .	2,823	2,772	2,743
U.K.—Total		421,177	422,059	420,353

Source: *Stock Exchange Yearbook.*

(v) The British Bankers' Association figures of advances, which show advances to local authorities quarterly. The February figures have been used, as the nearest available date to our other sources. They were:

	£m.
1953 . .	77·1
1954 . .	86·2
1955 . .	102·8

A complete reconciliation of these various sources is not possible. We did, however, take the gross loan debt of London, the counties and county boroughs, boroughs and urban districts and distribute it in the proportions shown in the I.M.T.A. return. This gave figures which corresponded closely with the known amount of stock and with our own estimate of internal advances. The figures for advances from the Public Works Loans Board and from banks were too low, which is not surprising as the sample was rather weak in the smaller authorities. No independent estimate is possible for mortgages and other debt.

In compiling our estimate of total liabilities we have taken the *Stock Exchange Yearbook* estimate of outstanding stock; the outstanding advances of the Public Works Loans Board; loans under the Land Settlement Acts, and the Building Materials and Housing Act, 1945, shown in the Finance Accounts; our own estimate of internal advances; and the British Bankers' Association figures for overdrafts. The remaining liabilities were assumed to be distributed between mortgages and other debt in the proportions indicated by the I.M.T.A. return. The results are shown in Table 24, and the consolidated balance-sheet for the local authorities in Table 25.

TABLE 24

Liabilities of local authorities

£ m. at 31 March

	1953	*1954*	*1955*
1. Quoted securities	560	575	580
2. Advances from Public Works Loans Board	2,215	2,496	2,828
3. Land Settlement and Housing and Building Materials Act	12	12	10
4. Internal loans	178	194	205
5. Bank overdrafts	77	86	103
6. Mortgages	456	584	639
7. Other debt	72	91	100
Total gross loan debt	3,571	4,038	4,465

Table 25 eliminates sinking funds, internal advances, and holdings of quoted local authority securities, so as to show the true position of local authorities as a whole in relation to other sectors. By far the largest part of the authorities' assets are, of course, the real assets already discussed, with a book-

TABLE 25

Consolidated balance-sheet of local authorities, 31 March 1953–5

£ m.

Liabilities	*1953*	*1954*	*1955*	*Assets*	*1953*	*1954*	*1955*
1. To central government	2,227	2,507	2,838	3. Real assets	3,293	3,751	4,171
2. To other sectors:				4. Financial assets:			
(*a*) Quoted securities (less internal holdings)	511	522	524	(*a*) Government securities	152	165	174
(*b*) Bank overdrafts	77	86	103	(*b*) Other securities	35	38	41
(*c*) Mortgages and other debt	528	675	739	(*c*) Cash	19	21	21
(*d*) Superannuation	290	314	340	(*d*) Loans under Small Dwellings Acquisition Acts	76	96	131
(*e*) Reserves	59	64	72	(*e*) Liabilities of public corporations and regional hospital boards for nationalized services	163	149	132
(*f*) Other special funds	44	51	53				
Total	3,738	4,220	4,670	Total	3,738	4,220	4.670

value of nearly £3,300 m. in 1953 and nearly £4,200 m. in 1955. They also had several hundred millions of financial assets which were claims on other sectors, of which the most important were government securities and loans to purchasers of houses under the Small Dwellings Acquisition Acts. Nearly two-thirds of local authorities' investment has been financed by loans from the central government, of which all but a trivial amount have come through the medium of the Public Works Loans Board. Under the Public Works Loans Act of 1945, local authorities were, in general, forbidden to borrow other than through the Public Works Loans Board. The relevant clause of this Act expired at the end of 1952, and thereafter there were some new issues of quoted securities, and a considerable increase in borrowing on mortgage. Local authority pension schemes, unlike those of the central government, are funded and, therefore, included in our reckoning of assets and liabilities. The authorities also have some liabilities in respect of trust, insurance, and other special funds. In all these cases the funds are partly invested in claims on other sectors and partly (as shown in Table 18) used internally.

APPENDIX TO CHAPTER 4

The value of local authority housing built since 1918 has been estimated by an alternative method based on that of Mr. Phillip Redfern.[1] For the years 1919–50 gross capital investment at current prices was derived by multiplying the number of houses built by local authorities[2] by an assumed 'representative price'. For 1925–38 inclusive, the price was that of a three-bedroom non-parlour local-authority house, including a charge for land and mains services, as given by Dr. M. Bowley.[3] For 1919–24 and 1939–50 this series was extrapolated by using Mr. Redfern's index of new housing.[4] This

[1] 'Net investment in Fixed Assets in the United Kingdom, 1938–53', *J.R.S.S.*, series A, part ii, 1955, pp. 141–81.

[2] E. D. Simon, *Rebuilding Britain; a Twenty Year Plan*, 1945, p. 255, for 1919–38; *Statistical Digest of the War*, H.M.S.O. 1951, p. 55, for 1939–45; returns of Ministry of Housing and Local Government for later years.

[3] M. Bowley, *Housing and the State*, 1945, p. 278.

[4] Redfern, op. cit., p. 271.

TABLE 26

Capital value of local authority housing (alternative estimate)

Year	Estimated no. of houses built	Assumed price	Gross fixed investment	Gross fixed investment at 1953 prices	Depreciation Over 100 yrs.	Depreciation Over 60 yrs.
		£	£m.	£m.	£m.	£m.
1919	432	754	0·3	0·6	0·2	0·3
1920	12,734	865	11·0	17·8	5·9	9·8
1921	69,130	754	52·1	96·5	30·9	51·5
1922	71,942	443	31·9	100·5	31·2	51·9
1923	31,455	455	14·3	43·9	13·2	21·9
1924	22,793	455	10·4	32·0	9·3	15·5
1925	43,096	510	22·0	60·3	16·9	28·1
1926	75,163	510	38·3	104·9	28·3	47·2
1927	111,299	481	53·5	156·8	40·8	67·9
1928	82,311	432	35·6	112·1	28·0	46·7
1929	72,370	416	30·1	99·8	24·0	39·9
1930	63,794	411	26·2	89·2	20·5	34·2
1931	72,555	404	29·3	102·5	22·6	37·6
1932	69,180	375	25·9	96·0	20·2	33·6
1933	69,368	362	25·1	93·0	18·6	31·0
1934	74,057	361	26·7	98·9	18·8	31·5
1935	71,696	371	26·6	101·6	18·3	30·5
1936	83,188	384	31·9	114·8	19·5	32·5
1937	90,891	427	38·8	125·4	20·1	33·4
1938	114,252	438	50·0	165·8	24·9	41·4
1939	87,370	461	40·3	126·9	17·8	29·6
1940	34,643	519	18·0	50·4	6·6	10·9
1941	10,751	576	6·9	17·4	2·1	3·5
1942	4,834	645	3·1	7·0	0·8	1·3
1943	4,965	726	3·6	7·2	0·7	1·2
1944	4,842	818	4·0	7·1	0·6	1·1
1945	2,544	922	2·3	3·6	0·3	0·5
1946	25,013	991	24·8	36·3	2·5	4·2
1947	97,340	1,083	105·4	141·3	8·5	14·1
1948	180,368	1,153	208·0	262·1	13·1	21·8
1949	165,946	1,176	195·2	241·1	9·6	16·1
1950	163,670	1,210	198·0	237·6	7·1	11·9
1951	162,582	1,550	294·8	317·5	6·4	10·6
1952	193,260	1,459	355·3	355·3	3·6	5·9
1953	238,883	1,407	423·5	423·5	..	..
Total	2,678,717	24,304	2,463·2	4,046·7	491·9	819·1

Estimated net capital value depreciating over 100 years, 3,554·8 £m.
Estimated net capital value depreciating over 60 years, 3,227·6 £m.

method probably understates the value of investment in the early post-war years because of the raising of local authorities' housing standards. For 1951–3 gross capital investment in housing by the public sector was taken from the 1957 *Economic Survey*[1] and adjusted for houses built by public agencies other than local authorities.

The figures for investment at current prices were then converted to 1953 prices by Mr. Redfern's index. Depreciation was allowed for on a 'straight-line' basis, first assuming a life of 100 years, as does Mr. Redfern, and secondly assuming a life of 60 years, the period over which local authorities normally provide for the amortization of their loans. The results are shown in Table 26. The value of houses at the end of 1953 is approximately £3,550 m. depreciating over 100 years and £3,230 m. depreciating over 60 years. Mr. Redfern's figure for all houses in the United Kingdom, adjusted to 1953 prices, is £12,850 m., so that local authorities appear to own about 28 per cent. of all houses by value. Numerically they own rather under a quarter of all houses,[2] but as the average age of local authority houses is much lower than that of houses in private ownership, the value figure appears not unreasonable.

The value £3,230 m. obtained by depreciating over 60 years compares with a net loan debt in respect of housing of £2,290 m. in 1953. This is an indication of the very large differences that can arise, in a period of inflation, between valuations based on present cost and those based on actual cost.

[1] Cmnd. 394, H.M.S.O. 1957.

[2] *Rent Control, Statistical Information*, Cmnd. 17, 1956, gives figures for Great Britain showing 3·5 m. houses publicly owned out of a total of 15·0 m.

5

THE PUBLIC SECTOR AS A WHOLE

THE consolidated statements at the end of the last three chapters have, so far as possible, eliminated transactions between different members of the same sector. This short chapter carries the process a stage farther by regarding the three public sectors as one and considering its relation to the rest of the economy. This involves the elimination of a further large group of cross-transactions. The items eliminated are shown in Table 27 and the consolidated statement *vis-à-vis* the rest of the economy in Table 28.

By 1955 the central government had lent over £800 m. directly to public corporations; government agencies held £726 m. of public corporations' stock in published accounts; and the corporations had tax liabilities of £59 m. No doubt there were also substantial amounts of public corporations' stock in unpublished accounts, especially in the Issue Department of the Bank, of which it is impossible to take account. However, in so far as the unpublished accounts held the securities of public corporations, they will have held correspondingly less of the national debt, so that this omission does not affect the estimate of total public sector liabilities to the rest of the economy.

The central government also held, in 1955, over £2,880 m. of local authority debt, composed almost entirely of loans through the Public Works Loans Board; holdings of local authority securities in published government accounts were trivial and it is most unlikely that any significant amount of these securities was held in unpublished accounts. Advances to local authorities stand at a higher figure in the books of the central government than in those of the local authorities, due to the issue of local loans at a discount. The central government accounts show the nominal value of the stock created, whereas those of local

TABLE 27. *Items eliminated in compiling the consolidated statement for the public sector*

Liabilities	*1953* £m.	*1954* £m.	*1955* £m.	*Assets*	*1953* £m.	*1954* £m.	*1955* £m.
			CENTRAL GOVERNMENT				
1. Securities held by:				11. Liabilities of public corporations:			
(*a*) Local authorities	152	165	174	(*a*) Loans	621	683	806
(*b*) Public corporations	100	89	142	(*b*) Securities held by departments	664	639	728
2. Liabilities to local authorities for transferred services	19	17	16	(*c*) Taxation interest and dividends	64	83	71
				12. Liabilities of local authorities	2,280	2,553	2,879
Total	271	271	332	Total	3,629	3,958	4,484
			PUBLIC CORPORATIONS				
3. Liabilities to central government	1,349	1,405	1,605	13. Central government securities	100	89	142
4. Adjustment	−39	10	−38	14. Loans to local authorities	6	9	20
	1,310	1,415	1,567	15. Deficiencies, &c.	168	136	166
5. Liability to local authorities for transferred services	138	125	112				
6. Reserves, deferred liabilities, and provisions	346	324	375				
Total	1,794	1,864	2,054	Total	274	234	328
			LOCAL AUTHORITIES				
7. Loans from central government	2,275	2,548	2,875	16. Liabilities for transferred services:			
8. Adjustment	−48	−41	−37	(*a*) Central government	19	17	16
	2,227	2,507	2,838	(*b*) Public corporations	138	125	112
9. Securities held by:				(*c*) Adjustment	5	7	4
(*a*) Departments of central government	5	5	4		162	149	132
(*b*) Public corporations	6	9	20	17. Government securities	152	165	174
10. Reserves, &c.	103	115	125				
Total	2,341	2,636	2,987	Total	314	314	306

Table 28

The public sector consolidated statement of assets and liabilities

£ m.

Liabilities	*1953*	*1954*	*1955*
1. Central government:			
(*a*) Internal debt	17,663	18,438	18,437
External debt	3,020	2,904	2,736
Savings bank deposits	2,752	2,738	2,770
Notes and coin	1,664	1,736	1,858
Debt of trading agencies	100	103	42
	25,199	25,919	25,843
2. Public corporations:			
(*b*) Securities	2,086	2,281	2,356
Other capital liabilities	169	174	181
Current liabilities	514	455	560
	2,769	2,910	3,097
3. Local authorities:			
(*c*) Securities	506	517	520
Mortgages and other debt	522	666	719
Overdrafts	77	86	103
Superannuation	290	314	340
	1,395	1,583	1,682
Total	29,363	30,412	30,622

£ m.

Assets	*1953*	*1954*	*1955*
Real assets:			
(*a*) Central Government (Ch. 2, Table 8)	1,430	1,435	1,323
(*b*) Public corporations (Ch. 3, Table 15)	3,563	3,844	4,104
(*c*) Local authorities (Ch. 4, Table 25)	3,293	3,751	4,171
	8,286	9,030	9,598
Liabilities of Domestic Private Sector:			
(*a*) Central government	1,309	1,278	1,330
(*b*) Public corporations	710	665	686
(*c*) Local authorities	95	117	152
	2,114	2,060	2,168
Liabilities of External Sector:			
(*a*) Central government	1,297	1,604	1,665
(*b*) Public corporations	13	21	18
(*c*) Local authorities	35	38	41
	1,345	1,663	1,724
Excess of liabilities over assets	17,618	17,659	17,132
Total	29,363	30,412	30,622

authorities show money received, less repayments. The difference is being amortized out of the excess income of the Local Loans Fund (the difference between the interest paid by the government and that charged by local authorities). This difference is shown in the 'adjustment' item for local authorities in Table 27.

The liabilities of the public corporations to the central government, as shown in their balance-sheets, do not coincide exactly with the corresponding assets in the *Finance Accounts*. This is mainly due to differences in accounting dates, especially in the cases of the National Coal Board and the Raw Cotton Commission. The difference is again shown in an 'adjustment' item in Table 27. Besides their liabilities to the central government, we have also eliminated the public corporations' liabilities to local authorities in respect of nationalized services, and their reserves, deferred liabilities, and provisions. The reserves of public corporations are an accounting item representing the excess of assets over other liabilities. Deferred liabilities and provisions cover a variety of items, which cannot be assigned to any particular sector, and many of which (such as internal insurance funds and actuarial deficiencies on pension funds) are contingent.

On the assets side of the balance-sheet we have eliminated the holdings of government securities by public corporations, their loans to local authorities, and deficiencies and goodwill. The goodwill item represents the excess of compensation paid over the book value of assets taken over, while deficiencies represent current losses financed by borrowing. Both items are, therefore, liabilities of the public sector against which there is no corresponding asset.

For local authorities we have, of course, eliminated loans from the Public Works Loans Board and the small amounts of loans and securities held by government departments and public corporations. We have also eliminated reserves and 'other special funds'. Some of the latter represent charitable and trust funds which should strictly be treated as liabilities to another sector but, without very detailed examination of the accounts of individual authorities, it is impossible to disentangle these.

On the assets side, the items eliminated are government securities and liabilities in respect of nationalized services, the latter again with a small adjustment for differences in accounting dates.

After taking out all these duplicate items, we are left with the consolidated statement of assets and liabilities shown in Table 28, which can be summarized very briefly. In 1955 the public sector as a whole owned real assets with a book value of over £9,500 m., the nature of which is described in previous chapters. It held over £1,300 m. of private sector liabilities consisting mainly of tax arrears, trade debts to public corporations, and loans by local authorities under the Small Dwellings Acquisition Acts. Finally, it held over £1,700 m. of liabilities of the external sector, composed mainly of reserves in the Exchange Equalization Account, and of central government loans to foreign countries.

On the other side of the account, the public sector had liabilities to other sectors of over £30,000 m. Of this, nearly £26,000 m. was on central government account (including £18,437 m. of internal debt and £2,770 m. of savings bank deposits), £3,097 m. on account of public corporations, and £1,682 m. on account of local authorities.

6

THE PERSONAL SECTOR

FOR obvious reasons, it is not possible to study the property of persons, as we have done for institutions, through the analysis of accounts. Three possible methods are available, estimation from sample surveys, from income-tax statistics, and from statistics of death duties. The first, which has been used to a considerable extent by the Oxford Institute of Statistics, involves field work of peculiar difficulty and would have been far beyond the resources available for this study. Income-tax statistics are also of limited use. Apart from the difficulties of capitalizing income discussed in Chapter 1, the schedules under which assessments are made and for which statistics are published bear little relationship to the categories of property which we require to distinguish. Moreover, there are difficulties about allowing for incomes below the exemption limit, and for income which does not accrue to the personal sector. We have, therefore, relied mainly upon the estate duty returns, which are analysed in some detail in the annual Inland Revenue reports.

The Reports give figures for the capital value of estates classified according to the age and sex of the deceased, and the basic method is to 'gross up' the capital value of estates in each age-sex group by the reciprocal of an appropriate specific mortality rate. In this way an estimate is obtained of the property held by living persons in each age-sex group. These can then be added to give an estimate for the whole community, and this can be distributed among different types of property in the proportion which each formed of estates liable to duty. The Inland Revenue statistics refer to estates on which duty was paid during the financial year. There is a time-lag, which may vary considerably from case to case, between death and payment of duty. We have assumed, however, that the figures for 1953–4 give a fair picture of the estates of persons dying in 1953, and similarly for later years.

The method, however, involves a number of difficulties. First, there is the choice of an appropriate specific mortality rate. A rate which is simply the ratio of deaths in any age-sex group to living persons in the group would be too high, as property owners have a better expectation of life than the population in general. The Registrar-General's decennial supplement, 1957, gives death rates for five social classes as a proportion of the rate for all classes for the years 1949–53.[1] There is no means of assigning property owners to any particular social class but it seemed likely that an overwhelmingly large proportion of substantial property owners would be included in either class I or class II. For estates of over £3,000 we therefore took the mean of the social class I and II rates weighted according to the number in each class in the 1957 census.[2] The decennial supplement gives separate rates for married and single women, and we used a weighted average of these as well as of the two social classes. In our estimate of estates below £3,000 we used the all classes death rate.

The exemption limit for estate duty was raised from £2,000 to £3,000 in the 1954 Finance Act for deaths occurring after 29 July 1954. However, the 1954–5 Inland Revenue Report gives statistics of estates above £2,000 for that year, even though they were not liable to duty. It is necessary, therefore, to estimate the value of estates under £2,000 for 1953–4 and 1954–5 and of estates under £3,000 for 1955–6.

It was assumed that all estates for which grants of representation were issued had a value of more than £100. This assumption is rather arbitrary, but inquiries among a number of people with experience in the field led us to believe that very small estates are generally disposed of without the formality of a grant. The number of estates between £100 and £2,000 or £3,000 was thus assumed to be the difference between the total number

[1] The Registrar-General's *Decennial Supplement, England and Wales*, 1957 Occupational Mortality, Part ii, vol. i, London, H.M.S.O., 1958, p. 23.

[2] *Census of England and Wales*, London, H.M.S.O., Occupational Tables, p. 149.

of grants of representation and the number of estates above the limit.[1] The numbers of estates in each range above the limit were plotted against the mean of the range in a cumulative frequency diagram, and the resulting curve produced so as to enable us to allocate the small estates, by extrapolation into a number of sub-groups in the range between £100 and the exemption limit. The estimated number of estates in each sub-group was then multiplied by the mean of its range, and the results totalled to give our estimate of the total value. The results were as follows:

	£*m.*
1953–4 (under £2,000) . .	5,394
1954–5 " " . .	6,190
1955–6 (under £3,000) . .	8,720

The method is clearly liable to a considerable margin of error, but even a large proportionate error would make only a modest difference to the estimate of total personal property. It is not possible to make any sort of estimate of the value of estates for which no grant of representation was issued, though we hazard a guess later for certain types of asset which seem particularly likely to have been held by persons of very small means.

A further set of difficulties arises in connexion with valuation. Valuation for probate is supposed to be on a basis of market value at date of death, though in some cases (notably interests in private companies) this is a very difficult concept to apply. Adjustments are, therefore, necessary in order to fit in with the basis of valuation used for other sectors, and these are discussed in connexion with each item later.

The basic assumption underlying the whole method is, of course, that the persons whose estates are liable to death duties in any year are a representative sample of all persons living. The sample may at times be distorted by the appearance of one or two large estates in the lower age groups, where deaths are few. A more serious possibility of error arises from the influence of age on the type of property held. Our method depends for its

[1] Figures of grants of representation are not available for Scotland. It was, therefore, assumed that the value of estates below the limit in Scotland bore the same proportion to the value of estates above the limit as in England and Wales.

accuracy on the proportions of different types of property being the same for all age groups. Suppose, however, that a particular type of property was held mainly by young people. If the amounts in each age group were known, each could be multiplied by its appropriate specific mortality rate, and a correct estimate could be obtained. In the absence of such knowledge we should, in effect, assume an even spread over all age groups. Hence, too, much of this particular type of property would be subject to too low a multiplier, and we should underestimate its amount. Conversely, of course, property held mainly by older people would be overestimated.

Since our own estimates were completed further work on this aspect of the subject has been done by Mr. J. R. S. Revell at the Department of Applied Economics at Cambridge. Mr. Revell has obtained hitherto unpublished information enabling him to estimate the amount of each type of asset held by persons dying in each age group separately, and so to multiply each by the correct specific mortality rate. Mr. Revell has kindly let me see his preliminary results for the year 1957–8, and these reveal important differences in some items. For shares in private companies, an estimate by his method yields a figure more than double ours. The differences for other assets are much less than this but Mr. Revell's method yields a considerably higher figure for trade assets, and lower ones for government and municipal securities, shares in public companies, mortgages, and cash.

No allowance is made for evasion and, so far as this occurs, it will result in an underestimate. The avoidance of duty by gifts *inter vivos* does not, however, lead to underestimation. The persons to whom property is transferred run the same risk of dying as others in their age-sex group, so that an appropriate fraction of transferred property will come under assessment due to the death of its new owners. Indeed, since gifts *inter vivos* are assessed with the estate of the donor if he or she dies within a certain time, a part of transferred property is subject to a double risk, so that the practice actually results in a slight overestimate.

Our estimates as derived from the Estate Duty Returns are

TABLE 29

Estimated assets of persons on basis of estate duty returns

£ *m.*

	1953	*1954*	*1955*
ANALYSIS OF PERSONALTY (excluding leaseholds):			
Government and municipal securities:			
British government securities . .	5,873	6,175	6,089
British municipal securities . .	283	265	259
Dominion securities, government and municipal	344	302	264
Foreign securities, government and municipal	90	87	76
Proprietary shares or debentures in joint stock, &c. companies:			
British companies (private) . .	1,963	1,898	1,894
British companies (public) . .	6,143	7,037	7,983
Dominion companies . . .	438	488	599
Foreign companies. . . .	107	136	138
Money out on mortgage of real estate in:			
Great Britain.	500	476	438
Dominions	4	4	..
Foreign countries	..	..	..
Shares and deposits in building societies, &c.	1,811	2,121	2,318
Other debts due to deceased . .	451	386	389
Household goods, &c. . . .	746	654	648
Insurance policies	836	847	858
Cash:			
In the house	53	49	45
At the bank	4,594	4,802	5,034
Trade, business, and professional assets:			
Plant, machinery, and fixed assets .	41	45	27
Patent rights and copyrights . .	..	..	..
Book debts	139	102	107
Farming stock	234	189	170
Stock other than farming . .	139	113	89
Goodwill, including trademarks .	123	102	94
Unallocated share of partnership. .	328	231	272
Ships or shares of ships . . .	4	4	4
Expectant interests (under will or settlement)	250	227	250
Share of deceased in personalty of an estate, so far as not apportionable among other items . . .	238	117	179
Cessers of annuities . . .	102	95	89
Proceeds of sale of settled realty, &c. .	98	64	63

TABLE 29 (*continued*)

£ *m.*

	1953	*1954*	*1955*
Income due, i.e. rents, profits, dividends, and interest	234	193	210
Not classified	70	68	85
Total gross capital value	26,236	27,277	28,671
ANALYSIS OF REALTY (including leaseholds)			
Land:			
Freehold	828	820	853
Copyhold or feudal	82	87	98
Leasehold	4	4	4
Buildings:			
Freehold	4,221	4,099	4,369
Copyhold or feudal	406	389	447
Leasehold	537	537	429
Mines, minerals, and quarries	4	4	4
Timber	37	38	36
Rents	127	129	147
Sporting rights	4	4	4
Cessers of annuities	12	−4	..
Expectant interests	4	4	9
Not classified	..	4	4
Total gross capital value	6,266	6,115	6,404
Total, personalty and realty	32,502	33,391	35,075

shown in Table 29, while Table 30 shows the figures rearranged and modified so as to bring them as far as possible into line with our estimates for other sectors. The main changes involved in this are discussed below.

British government securities

These comprise quoted securities (including guaranteed stocks), national savings certificates, and defence bonds. These 'small savings' securities are, of course, intended for the personal holder. We have found some in the balance-sheets of churches, charities, sports clubs, and even universities, but their appearance is rare, and the amounts are small. The Post Office Savings Department has informed us that it believes 'the vast majority' of these securities to be in personal hands, but it is unable to give a firm figure.

A sample inquiry among persons undertaken by the Social Survey for the National Savings Committee, when grossed up, accounted for 110 per cent. of the total issue of savings certificates and 87 per cent. of that of defence bonds.[1] The Oxford survey conducted by Mr. H. M. Lydall traced 70 per cent. of savings certificates and 74 per cent. of defence bonds to personal ownership.[2] This survey, however, did not cover the whole population and Mr. Lydall suggests that the sections excluded might, at a maximum, hold 25 per cent. of assets. We have,

TABLE 30. *The assets of the personal sector*

£ *m.*

	1953	*1954*	*1955*
1. British government securities:			
(*a*) Quoted securities	3,626	3,783	3,769
(*b*) National savings	2,440	2,421	2,490
(*c*) Post-war credits	581	564	520
2. Public corporations	744	741	773
3. Local authorities and public boards	316	283	286
4. British companies:			
(*a*) Public	6,076	6,961	7,903
(*b*) Private	1,942	1,878	1,875
5. Overseas securities:			
(*a*) Government and municipal	429	385	336
(*b*) Companies	539	618	730
6. Mortgages and other debts	1,082	958	925
7. Real assets:			
(*a*) Fixed capital	7,185	6,906	7,155
(*b*) Stocks	1,471	1,523	1,596
8. Life assurance policies	2,568	2,745	2,973
9. Pension rights	1,379	1,594	1,808
10. Building societies and Co-operative societies	1,875	2,357	2,405
11. Cash:			
(*a*) Commercial banks	2,243	2,335	2,429
(*b*) P.O., Trustee, and railway savings banks	2,885	2,894	2,975
(*c*) Notes and coin	175	184	195
12. Other assets	1,223	925	1,087
Total	38,779	40,055	42,230

[1] *The Public and National Savings.* National Savings Committee, 1948.

[2] National Survey of Personal Incomes and Savings, *Bulletin of the Oxford University Institute of Statistics,* June–July 1953.

therefore, assumed that 5 per cent. of savings certificates and defence bonds were owned other than by persons.

It is also necessary to allow for holdings of small savings in estates of less than £100, and for the probable underestimate of government securities in estates between £100 and the exemption limit. The National Savings Committee survey found that 59 per cent. of the adult population held some national savings, and Mr. Lydall found the same for 56 per cent. of his 'income units'. The National Savings Committee found that 81·6 per cent. of national savings were owned by persons with total holdings of under £2,000, 55 per cent. in holdings of under £1,000 and 37·8 per cent. in holdings of under £500. Of course, many comparatively small holders of national savings would have held other assets which would have raised their total estates above the exemption limit. We have assumed that 5 per cent. of national savings were held in estates of under £100 and a further 35 per cent. in estates of under £2,000.

The allowance for estates under £100 has to be added to our estimate of total personal property. The assumption about estates between £100 and £2,000 implies that, as one might expect, small estates held a higher proportion of government securities than larger ones. If small estates had held government securities in the same proportion as larger ones, they would have accounted for only about £860 m. of government securities, yet our allowance of 35 per cent. of small savings would, in itself, account for about £900 m. Small estates obviously hold some government securities other than national savings, and we have assumed that these are a quarter of total holdings.

If estates of less than £2,000 hold a more than average proportion of government securities they must, of course, hold a smaller proportion of other assets. In allowing for this we have assumed that the reduction, compared to the average of all estates, is proportionally the same for all assets. The figures of Table 29 have been adjusted in this manner in Table 30.

Quoted securities are valued at market value on day of death. We have assumed that holdings are evenly spread over the whole range of quoted stock, and have estimated nominal values using the difference between nominal and market value for the whole debt at 31 March as given in *The Stock Exchange Yearbook*. We have further assumed that holdings are distributed between the national debt and guaranteed stocks in proportion to the amounts in issue. This gives the following result:

Personal holdings of quoted gilt-edged
Estimated nominal values £ m.

National Debt			*Guaranteed stocks*		
1953	*1954*	*1955*	*1953*	*1954*	*1955*
3,626	3,783	3,769	744	741	773

Finally, post-war credits have been added to our estimated holding of government securities. This involves some double counting, as some of these credits will either appear in the estates of holders who die or will have been repaid before death and reinvested in some other asset that is held until death. It appeared likely, however, that a high proportion would be repaid and spent prior to death and so escape our previous reckoning.

Local authorities and public boards

All these securities are, of course, fixed interest and we have converted to nominal values using the *Stock Exchange Yearbook* valuations.

Overseas securities

In adjusting fixed-interest government and municipal stocks nominal value, we have used the *Stock Exchange Yearbook* figures for Dominion and Colonial stocks only. The Stock Exchange figures for foreign stocks include some that are now practically valueless, and hence the ratio of nominal to market values is very high. The use of this figure here would have given an estimate of personal holdings which was quite unrealistic.

Stocks

The figure derived from the estate duty returns is much lower than that of the National Income Blue Book. The estate duty method is likely to be unreliable for this asset and, in Table 30, we have used figures from the 1958 Blue Book.

Life-assurance policies

One item for which the estate-duty figures are entirely useless is insurance policies, since a large proportion of these are endowment policies which fall due before death. The value of insurance policies is, therefore, taken from the balance-sheets of the companies analysed in Chapter 8, with an adjustment for foreign business of British companies and policies held by British residents with foreign companies. Adding this figure to estimates of other types of property derived from the estate-duty returns involves an element of double-counting, since some holders of maturing endowment policies use the money to buy other forms of property, which they hold until death and which are eventually assessed for duty. Others, however, either convert their maturing policies into annuities or spend them, at some time before death, on consumption, and there is no means of knowing how much of maturing policies is used in either way.

Pension rights

Pension rights form a part of the assets of the personal sector which, for obvious reasons, is not reflected in the estate-duty returns. It has only been possible to take account of rights in funded schemes, and the value of pension rights is taken as that of the assets of these schemes.

Cash

The estate-duty returns distinguish between cash 'in the house' and 'in the bank'. When 'grossed up' these figures work out at only about £50 m. cash 'in the house'. That this estimate is absurdly low is hardly surprising. The temptation to relatives not to leave ready cash to fall into the hands of the tax collector is too strong to be resisted.

The estimate in Table 30 has been made on the assumption of an average holding of notes and coin equal to half a week's income for wage-earners, members of the armed forces, and recipients of national insurance and assistance; and to one week's income derived from salary, self-employment, rent, dividend, or interest.

The estimate of cash in the bank tallies rather better with other evidence. This item includes cash in the Post Office and Trustee and Railway savings banks, as well as in ordinary banks. The savings banks are, of course, used by charities, friendly societies, and clubs of various kinds as well as by persons, but all our evidence about these bodies suggests that non-personal holdings are small. In Table 30 we have assumed that all but £30 m. of savings bank deposits were in personal hands. Our estimates can be summarized as follows:

£*m.*

	1953	*1954*	*1955*
Personal savings bank deposits	2,885	2,894	2,975
Estimated deposits with commercial banks .	1,659	1,856	2,009
Total	4,544	4,750	4,984

An alternative estimate of commercial bank deposits can be compiled, starting with the figure of net personal deposits in the clearing banks at the end of 1950, given to the Royal Commission on Taxation. Adding or subtracting the change in net personal deposits given in the National Income Blue Book, making a proportionate adjustment for non-clearing banks, and adding personal and professional advances we get the following result:

£*m.*

	1953	*1954*	*1955*
Net personal deposits in clearing banks . .	1,789	1,869	1,945
Adjustment for non-clearing banks . . .	87	92	95
Personal and professional advances . . .	367	374	389
Total	2,243	2,335	2,429

This estimate should be lower than the previous one as the estate duty returns include non-corporate business, while the clearing banks excluded non-corporate business deposits as far as possible from their estimate of net personal deposits. Clearly the estate duty method leads to a substantial underestimate of cash in the bank as well as in the house. In Table 30 we have, therefore, used the estimate derived from the net personal deposits of the clearing banks. This is still too low by the amount of non-corporate business balances excluded by the banks in compiling their returns of personal deposits.

Other assets

This item, taken from the estate-duty estimates without any adjustment, comprises unallocated shares of partnerships, expectant interests, cessors of annuities, income due, share of personalty, and items unclassified by the Inland Revenue authorities.

The liabilities of the personal sector

Liabilities outstanding against an estate are, of course, deducted from its gross capital value in order to arrive at the net capital value on which duty is levied. The difference between gross and net capital values, however, does not form a basis for estimating liabilities. An estimate derived in the way we have used for assets is quite absurdly low. This is probably due to two reasons. First, liabilities tend to be concentrated among the small estates, since the rich man has normally no need to borrow, so that a large part of them are probably incurred by people with estates below the exemption limit. Secondly, liabilities tend to be incurred by people in early adult life and paid off before they reach old age. This is particularly true of mortgages for house purchase, which form a very important part of personal liabilities. This fact, for reasons already indicated, would cause our method to give a serious underestimate.

It is, therefore, necessary to fall back on indirect evidence, and we have assembled, in Table 31, the assets of other sectors which appear to be wholly or very largely liabilities of persons.

Nearly three-quarters of the total consists of mortgage loans from local authorities under the Small Dwellings Acquisition Acts (Chapter 4, Table 25); insurance companies (Chapter 9, Table 45); building societies (Chapter 9, Table 48); the Agricultural Mortgage Corporation; and other persons. We have assumed that all 'mortgages and other debts' held by persons (Table 30), and all the mortgages of the institutions named above, are liabilities of persons. Mortgages held by other institutions and by charities are assumed to be liabilities of local authorities. Building societies and insurance companies show their holdings of local authority loans separately, but some of their loans classified as mortgages may be the liabilities of companies. Also, some mortgages held by persons may be liabilities of companies or local authorities.

TABLE 31. *The liabilities of the personal sector*

£ m.

	1953	*1954*	*1955*
1. Mortgage loans from:			
(*a*) Local authorities	76	96	131
(*b*) Persons	1,082	958	925
(*c*) Insurance companies	362	396	430
(*d*) Building societies	1,396	1,574	1,752
(*e*) Agricultural Mortgage Corporation	24	26	26
	2,940	3,050	3,264
2. Bank loans and overdrafts	623	651	685
3. Hire-purchase debt	272	318	403
4. Other loans	78	82	88
5. Arrears of taxation	125	124	151
Total	4,038	4,225	4,591

Our figure for bank loans and overdrafts includes personal and professional advances, advances to farmers and stockbrokers, and estimated call loans to the stock exchange. It does not, however, include loans to non-corporate business in other sectors. Hire-purchase debt includes estimated liabilities to public corporations, companies, and finance houses, and 'other loans' comprises loans on policies by insurance companies and personal loans by co-operative societies. Arrears of taxation are estimated from the Inland Revenue reports as described in Chapter 2. They do not include tax liabilities currently incurred but not yet due. Other omissions are the trade debt of non-corporate business, debts to retailers other than hire-purchase, and arrears of rent and rates. Thus, while the table somewhat overestimated mortgage liabilities, it underestimates personal indebtedness to the banks, and, perforce, omits several significant items. On balance, it seems more likely to understate than to overstate total liabilities.

Summary

In 1955 persons had gross assets of over £42,000 m. and liabilities of between £4,000 and £5,000 m., so that the 'net worth' of the personal sector was something over £37,000 m. Only about £8,700 (20·8 per cent. of gross assets) was in tangible form, land and buildings, plant, equipment, and stocks, and the remainder consisted of various types of financial claim. Of these, nearly £7,000 m. were direct liabilities of the central government in the form of either quoted securities, small savings, post-war credits, or currency. There were over £2,975 m. of savings bank deposits backed almost entirely by government securities. Nearly £7,300 m. consisted of commercial bank deposits, insurance policies, and pension rights. Allowing for the proportion of government securities normally held by these institutions, we can estimate that about £12,500 m. or 30 per cent. of all personal assets vested either directly or at one remove on the liabilities of the central government. A further £1,100 m. of personal assets were in the securities of public corporations or local authorities, and a similar amount in overseas securities. The remaining large component in personal assets is the stocks and shares of joint-stock companies, which amounted to over £10,000 m.

7

NON-FINANCIAL COMPANIES

THE company sector is here taken to include all non-financial companies (including co-operative societies) operating mainly in the United Kingdom. Companies registered in Britain but operating mainly overseas are treated as part of the overseas sector, and British holdings in them as part of our foreign investments. In order to be consistent with our practice elsewhere, companies operating in Northern Ireland should have been treated as overseas companies, but the available statistics do not provide any basis for separating them.

Our knowledge of company finance has been greatly extended by the studies of the balance-sheets of quoted companies undertaken by the National Institute of Economic and Social Research and continued by the Board of Trade. There are still, however, many respects in which the statistics are defective and difficult to interpret.

PUBLIC COMPANIES

The following sources have been used here:

1. The returns of the Registrar of Joint Stock Companies which give, for the end of each year, the number of companies, both public and private, and the amount of their nominal share capital. The figures refer to nominal paid-up capital only, they do not include loan capital, and they do not, of course, distinguish between companies according either to the nature or the place of their operations.

2. The *Stock Exchange Yearbook*, which publishes an analysis of the number, nominal value, and market value of all securities quoted on the London Stock Exchange for 31 March of each year. This analysis divides securities into a number of groups according to the nature of their operations, but the classification

bears little relation to that used by the National Institute and the Board of Trade. In particular the large 'Commercial and Industrial' section includes many industrial groups. Equally serious defects are that the figures do not distinguish between debenture, preference, and ordinary capital; they do not distinguish between companies registered in Britain and abroad; and there is no specific distinction between companies operating at home and abroad, though this can often be inferred from the classification.

3. *Interest and Dividends on Securities Quoted on the London Stock Exchange*. This comparatively recent publication by the Council of the Stock Exchange adds considerably to the information contained in the *Yearbook*, though with some very awkward differences in date and coverage. The figures refer to 30 June or 31 December, whereas the corresponding ones in the *Yearbook* refer to 31 March. Estimates are given of nominal loan, preference share, and ordinary share capital: figures for loan capital refer to both British and foreign capital provided it has a sterling designation, but those for preference and ordinary shares refer only to companies registered and managed in the United Kingdom. Estimates of market value are given from the middle of 1954 onwards for a range of groups similar to (though slightly more limited than) those of the *Yearbook*. There is also an estimate of the proportion of quoted capital to the total capital of public companies. Investment trusts are not included.

The total number of companies included, together with the number of investment trusts, is appreciably greater than the number of companies in the Registrar's statistics (Table 32). It would appear, therefore, that the latter figures are not entirely comprehensive.

4. The analysis of balance-sheets undertaken by the Board of Trade, and published in *Economic Trends*. This provides most valuable information about a large part of the company sector. In the main, it is confined to quoted companies operating mainly in the United Kingdom, though a small number of large unquoted companies are included. Financial companies are, of

course, omitted and so are companies in shipping and agriculture and most of the oil companies, which are regarded as operating mainly abroad. The figures are, of course, obtained by adding balance-sheets for accounting dates distributed all through the calendar year.

With so many discrepancies in date, and coverage between these various sources, it is impossible to fit them into a picture that is entirely complete and consistent. They can, however, be made to throw a considerable amount of light on the situation.

TABLE 32

Registered companies with a share capital in existence at the end of the year

	Number		*Paid-up capital £m.*	
	Public	*Private*	*Public*	*Private*
1952	11,695	254,021	3,995	2,369
1953	11,553	261,981	4,088	2,391
1954	11,457	272,497	4,188	2,473
1955	11,312	283,321	4,375	2,515

Sources: *Registrar of Joint Stock Companies. Annual Abstract of Statistics*

In Table 32 we show the number and share capital of all companies from the Registrar's returns. Table 33 shows our estimate of the nominal capital of public companies which are quoted on the London Stock Exchange, derived from the *Yearbook* and *Interest and Dividends*. We have divided this capital between British and foreign companies, and British companies are further subdivided into non-financial companies operating mainly in the United Kingdom, financial companies operating mainly in the United Kingdom, and companies operating mainly abroad. The estimate of the capital of foreign companies was made by comparing the figures in the *Stock Exchange Yearbook*, which include foreign companies, with those in *Interest and Dividends*, which do not. This comparison was supplemented, where necessary, by an examination of the places of registration of companies, as given in the *Yearbook*. The division between financial and non-financial can be easily made by reference to the categories used in the Stock Exchange classification; following the procedure of the Board of Trade analysis and the National

TABLE 33

Estimated nominal share and loan capital of companies quoted on the London Stock Exchange

£ m. at mid-year

	1953				1954				1955			
	Deb.	*Pref.*	*Ord.*	*Total*	*Deb.*	*Pref.*	*Ord.*	*Total*	*Deb.*	*Pref.*	*Ord.*	*Total*
1. Non-financial companies operating in the U.K.	436	998	1,808	3,242	449	1,046	2,145	3,640	518	1,088	2,517	4,123
2. Financial companies operating in the U.K.	258	165	313	736	273	162	351	786	286	177	399	862
3. U.K. companies operating abroad	196	85	507	787	212	82	482	776	206	85	588	881
4. Total U.K. companies	889	1,248	2,628	4,765	935	1,290	2,977	5,202	1,010	1,352	3,504	5,866
5. Foreign companies				1,086				1,046				1,292
Total				5,851				6,248				7,158

Income Blue Book, property companies have been treated as part of the financial sector. The division between companies operating in the U.K. and abroad was also made mainly by reference to the Stock Exchange categories, though in some cases such as banks and property companies, the particulars of individual companies in the *Yearbook* were examined. Shipping companies are included in the United Kingdom sector, but oil companies are treated as operating abroad. Strictly, their U.K. refining and sales activities should, of course, be treated as part of the domestic sector, but it was impossible to separate the capital involved in these from that used in their overseas operations. On the other hand, the 'commercial and industrial' category has been treated as wholly domestic, though it includes a few companies whose activities are mainly overseas.

The figures of Table 33 are rather lower than those of Table 32 for 1953 but a little higher for 1954 and substantially higher for 1955. In view of the discrepancies between the number of companies in the Stock Exchange tabulation and in the Registrar's statistics, the 1954 and 1955 figures are not surprising.

Table 34 shows a similar estimate of the market value of the various classes of capital. The division between different categories was made in the same way as for Table 33. The valuations for 1954 and 1955 are based on *Interest and Dividends*. This publication, however, does not give any valuation prior to June 1954 so the figures for 1953 had to be derived from those for 1954 by using the Actuaries' Index of Ordinary Shares and the *Financial Times* index of fixed interest shares. The coverage of these indexes, is however, by no means the same as that of our table, so the 1953 figures may be subject to considerable error.

Between 1953 and 1955 the nominal value of the quoted capital of all British companies rose from £4,765 m. to £5,866 m., mainly because of a rise of £876 m. in ordinary shares. Only a small part of this increase was due to new capital issues; the remainder was due in small part to companies securing quotations for shares not previously quoted but mainly to the issue of bonus shares.

The main feature that emerges in comparing Tables 33 and 34

TABLE 34

Estimated market value of share and loan capital of companies quoted on the London Stock Exchange

£ m. at mid-year

	1953				1954				1955			
	Deb.	*Pref.*	*Ord.*	*Total*	*Deb.*	*Pref.*	*Ord.*	*Total*	*Deb.*	*Pref.*	*Ord.*	*Total*
1. Non-financial companies operating in the U.K. .	383	1,031	3,940	5,354	406	1,094	5,391	6,891	465	1,073	7,283	8,821
2. Financial companies operating in the U.K. . .	216	138	1,157	1,511	229	146	1,140	1,515	232	155	1,622	2,009
3. U.K. companies operating abroad	142	67	988	1,197	169	83	1,337	1,589	158	87	2,003	2,248
4. Total U.K. companies .	741	1,236	6,085	8,062	804	1,323	7,868	9,995	855	1,315	10,908	13,078
5. Foriegn companies . .				1,436				1,943				2,768
Total				9,498				11,938				15,846

is the magnitude of the rise in the market value of ordinary shares. In the middle of 1953 the market was only just beginning to pull out of the 1952 slump, while mid-1955 marked the peak of a boom. While there were only modest changes in the total value of debentures and preference shares, the ordinary shares of British companies rose in value by about £5,000 m.

The Board of Trade has kindly given me information about the balance-sheets of unquoted companies included in their survey, and the relevant figures have been subtracted from those published in *Economic Trends* to give a combined balance-sheet of quoted companies only, shown in Table 35.

Finally, in Table 36 we have compiled an estimated balance sheet for all non-financial public companies operating in the U.K., as defined for Table 33. In doing this, we made a separate estimate of the assets and liabilities of shipping companies from balance-sheet summaries in the *Stock Exchange Yearbook*. For other companies the figures for preference and ordinary shares from Table 33 were raised to allow for the unquoted capital of quoted companies and for all share capital of unquoted public companies (in the proportions given in *Interest and Dividends*. Loan capital was more difficult. *Interest and Dividends* gives no figure for the proportion of unquoted to quoted loan capital, but a comparison of Tables 33 and 35 makes it apparent that the amount shown in Table 33 (even allowing for differences in coverage between the two tables) is absurdly low. The reason is probably in the habit, believed to be fairly widespread among smaller companies, of 'placing' debentures privately without seeking a quotation. We therefore assumed that debentures bore the same proportion to share capital as in the companies analysed by the Board of Trade. The remaining items were then estimated on the assumption that they formed the same proportion of capital and reserves as in Table 35.

The assets of public companies appear to have risen by nearly 20 per cent. from £11,600 m. to £14,100 m. between 1953 and 1955. In 1955 fixed assets amounted to more than £5,250 m. and stocks to nearly £4,000 m. Trade debtors amounted to £2,678 m., cash to £785 m., and investments to £576 m.

TABLE 35

Public companies included in the Board of Trade analysis. Balance-sheet summary

Liabilities (£ m.)	*1953*	*1954*	*1955*	*Assets* (£ m.)	*1953*	*1954*	*1955*
Debentures	698	797	882	Fixed assets	3,326	3,702	4,153
Preference shares	854	900	919	Trade investments	226	236	250
Ordinary shares	1,787	2,154	2,415	Goodwill, &c.	249	254	258
				Unconsolidated subsidiaries	34	29	30
Total share and loan capital	3,339	3,851	4,216	Stocks and work in progress	2,871	3,089	3,443
Reserves	3,720	3,832	4,188	Trade and other debtors	1,804	2,011	2,285
Minority interests	264	296	306	Investments:			
Current liabilities:				Government securities	315	303	393
Bank overdrafts and loans	288	309	359	Other	37	35	58
Trade and other creditors	1,432	1,598	1,808	Tax reserve certificates	223	284	220
Dividends and interest due	132	157	170	Cash	809	805	691
Current taxation	622	617	643				
Provisions	92	89	90				
Total	9,889	10,749	11,780	Total	9,894	10,748	11,781

Source: *Economic Trends*, February 1958. The figures for private companies included in this analysis have been subtracted.

TABLE 36

Estimated assets and liabilities of non-financial public companies operating in the United Kingdom

£ m.

Liabilities	*1953*	*1954*	*1955*
1. Debentures	801	927	1,013
2. Preference shares	1,081	1,133	1,178
3. Ordinary shares	2,039	2,420	2,839
4. Total share and loan capital	3,921	4,480	5,030
5. Reserves	4,340	4,442	4,975
6. Minority interests	301	333	352
7. Current liabilities:			
(*a*) Bank overdrafts and loans	331	352	427
(*b*) Trade and other creditors	1,730	1,915	2,229
(*c*) Dividends and interest due	156	183	206
(*d*) Current taxation	736	722	768
(*e*) Provisions	111	106	112
Total	11,626	12,533	14,099

£ m.

Assets	*1953*	*1954*	*1955*
8. Fixed assets	4,082	4,476	5,251
9. Trade investments	240	251	271
10. Goodwill, &c.	281	292	296
11. Unconsolidated subsidiaries	37	33	34
12. Stocks and work in progress	3,254	3,512	3,944
13. Trade and other debtors	2,091	2,327	2,678
14. Investments:			
(*a*) Government securities	428	363	509
(*b*) Other	44	38	67
15. Tax reserve certificates	259	330	264
16. Cash	910	910	785
Total	11,626	12,533	14,099

The holding by one public company of shares in another appears to be comparatively small. Our examination of the balance-sheets tabulated by the National Institute of Economic and Social Research showed that items classed as 'investments' in balance-sheets were very largely government securities, though they also included modest amounts of local authority stocks and mortgages, and small amounts deposited with building societies. 'Unconsolidated subsidiaries', which are very small, have been assumed to be unquoted companies. 'Trade investments' have been assumed to be shares in quoted companies, though they may include some shares in unquoted ones. The amounts involved were £240 m. in 1953 and £270 m. in 1955. As a check on the reliability of this assumption, we examined the holdings of the hundred largest companies, as tabulated by the National Institute of Economic and Social Research. These companies, with a total capital of £3,307 m., held in 1953 approximately £82 m. (nominal) of the capital of other companies.

PRIVATE COMPANIES

The existing information about private companies is so slight as to be almost negligible. The only analysis of balance-sheets that we know of is that presented by the British Bankers' Association to the Royal Commission on Taxation. The survey covered about 1,500 private companies whose balance-sheets were in the hands of the banks, and showed their aggregate position for 1947 and 1949 or 1950.

The figures are as follows:

£ m. in 1949 or 1950

Liabilities		*Assets*	
Capital	56·2	Cash	9·0
Reserves	58·9	Marketable securities	5·2
Bank overdraft	30·6	Debtors and bills receivable	65·5
Creditors and bills payable	69·4	Stocks	90·6
		Other assets	44·9
Total	215·1	Total	215·1

The sample was, however, unrepresentative in two ways. The companies concerned were much above average in size with an average nominal capital of over £37,000 compared with only about £11,000 for all private companies in the Registrar's returns. They were also companies which had been recent borrowers from the banks.

Had the sample been representative one could, of course, estimate any one balance-sheet item for all private companies and then build up the rest of the balance-sheet on the basis of the sample. There are three possible items that can be used in this way—capital, taken from the Registrar's returns; stocks, the difference between stocks held by public companies and the figure for all companies in the National Income Blue Book; and bank overdrafts which can be estimated, though only very roughly, from the classified advances of the British Bankers' Association. We tried each of these methods, but the results not only differed very widely from one another, but also checked very badly with other sources of information. We were forced, therefore, to conclude that the sample was too unrepresentative to give a useful guide to the position of private companies as a whole.

Private companies have about 37 per cent. of the nominal capital of all companies as shown in the Registrar's returns, but they appear to earn slightly under 30 per cent. of all company profits. This discrepancy is not surprising as the figures for capital include the nominal capital of private companies which are subsidiaries of public companies, and whose accounts would be consolidated with those of their parents. In Table 37 we have assumed that items other than share capital and reserves form three-sevenths of the corresponding estimates for public companies; share capital has been taken from the Registrar's returns, and 'reserves' are the balancing item.

This is a very crude and unsatisfactory form of guesswork but, until it is possible to examine a truly random sample of balance-sheets, there seems to be no alternative.

CO-OPERATIVE SOCIETIES

The co-operative societies make statistical returns to the Chief Registrar of Friendly Societies.[1] In Table 38 we have estimated

[1] *Annual Reports of the Chief Registrar of Friendly Societies*, Part iii.

TABLE 37. *Estimated assets and liabilities of private companies*

Liabilities	£ m. 1953	1954	1955	*Assets*	£ m. 1953	1954	1955
1. Capital	2,723	2,829	2,928	7. Fixed assets	1,749	1,918	2,250
2. Reserves	885	1,073	1,448	8. Stocks	1,395	1,505	1,690
3. Bank overdrafts	142	151	183	9. Trade debtors	896	997	1,148
4. Trade creditors	741	821	955	10. Investments	202	172	247
5. Current taxation	315	309	329	11. Tax reserve certificates	111	141	113
6. Other liabilities	177	188	199	12. Cash	390	390	336
	4,983	5,371	6,042	13. Other assets	240	248	258
Total	4,983	5,371	6,042	Total	4,983	5,371	6,042

TABLE 38. *The Assets and liabilities of co-operative societies*

Liabilities	£ m. 1953	1954	1955	*Assets*	£ m. 1953	1954	1955
1. Shares	223	226	231	5. Fixed assets	109	110	115
2. Loans and deposits	64	60	58	6. Stocks	99	100	103
3. Reserves	33	35	37	7. Debtors	20	20	24
4. Sundry funds[1]	42	45	51	8. Investments	87	88	86
				9. Cash	40	41	45
				10. Other assets	6	6	4
Total	362	366	376	Total	362	366	376

[1] These include a number of small funds but are mainly the assets of employees' saving and pension funds.

the assets and liabilities of the retail, wholesale, and productive societies. The English and Scottish C.W.S. banks and the Co-operative Insurance Society are included with banks and insurance companies, respectively, and so are excluded here. We have also cut out duplication between the wholesale and retail societies, of which there is a great deal in the published figures. In making these adjustments we have been greatly helped by information supplied by the Co-operative Wholesale Society, the Scottish Co-operative Wholesale Society, and the Co-operative Union.

SUMMARY

Anything we say about the assets and liabilities of the company sector as a whole must be said with great diffidence because of the gap in our knowledge of private companies. It would appear, however, that non-financial companies engaged mainly in British industry and trade had fixed assets in 1955 of around £7,500 m. book value. These book values are normally based on cost less depreciation, and valuation on a replacement cost basis would, of course, give a considerably higher figure. Though companies operating mainly abroad have, as far as possible, been excluded, there are a number of companies whose main business is in Britain but who have foreign branches or subsidiaries. If these are consolidated with the parent, their assets would appear in the balance-sheets on which Table 36 is founded. Hence a part of our £7,500 m. represents fixed assets held abroad rather than at home.

Stocks and work in progress come out in our estimate at over £5,700 m. This is higher than the estimate in the National Income Blue Book of £5,597 m. at the end of 1955 and £5,117 m. at the end of 1954. There is, however, a discrepancy between the Blue Book figures and the Board of Trade balance-sheet summaries. The former suggests a rise in the value of stocks for all companies of only about £500 m. from mid-1953 to mid-1955, whereas the companies in the Board of Trade analysis alone increased their stocks by £592 m. It is hard to believe that other companies were reducing their stocks during this period, so the Blue Book figure may well need revision.

Trade investments are, of course, liabilities of one company to another, and the same is largely true of trade debtors, which amount to over £3,800 m. The other main assets of companies that are liabilities of other sectors are investments, tax reserve certificates, and cash. Investments, mostly government securities, amounted to about £900 m.; tax reserve certificates are subject to considerable seasonal fluctuation, averaging around £350 m. but dropping well below this at the beginning of the year; finally, cash appears to amount to over £1,150 m.

The main liabilities that form the counterpart to these assets are, of course, those to companies' own shareholders, over £8,000 m. of share and loan capital and £6,000 m. of reserves. Trade creditors amounted to £450 m. less than trade debtors for public companies, i.e. these companies were giving net credits of £450 m. either to private companies or to other sectors. The assumptions on which we have drawn up Table 37 necessarily show private companies also as net creditors under this heading. The British Bankers' Association shows a slight net debtor position but the sample is particularly unrepresentative here; the companies concerned had a very high level of stocks and had been adding to them very rapidly. Their stocks in 1949–50 were nearly double their nominal capital and more than double their fixed assets, and they had more than doubled in the three years since 1946. It would be only natural that firms in this very unusual stock position should make much more than average use both of bank loans and trade credit. Indeed, the fact that even these companies were net debtors only to a small extent makes it seem quite plausible to assume that private companies as a whole were net creditors.

Our estimate of bank overdrafts (£610 m. in 1958) is less than one would expect from the analysis of advances discussed in Chapter 8. This is again probably due to our treatment of private companies. It is inconceivable that all private companies should borrow as much, in relation to their capital, as do those in the B.B.A. sample. On the other hand, it seems highly probable that they borrow to a greater extent than public companies, so that the figure for this item in Table 37 is almost certainly an underestimate.

8

THE BANKING SYSTEM

THE aim of this and the following chapter is to analyse the available information about the group of institutions which may be collectively called the capital market. In the present chapter we discuss institutions whose main business is the making of short-term loans, and which derive a large part of their funds from loans or deposits repayable on demand or at short notice. They are the London clearing banks, the Scottish banks, a group of other banks, the merchant banks or accepting houses, and the discount houses. All these institutions, together with others, are included in the financial companies sub-sector of the National Income Blue Book. The line between them and other near-banking institutions such as savings banks and hire-purchase finance houses, is, at times, a narrow one. However, this group is so closely linked together by tradition and by its close association through the London money market that it seems reasonable to treat it as a whole.

THE CLEARING BANKS AND THE SCOTTISH BANKS

The London clearing banks publish monthly statements of the principal classes of their assets and liabilities, in addition to their end-year balance-sheets. The Scottish banks do not publish these figures, and the only information about their position is contained in their annual balance-sheets; moreover, these balance-sheets are made up at different dates.[1] In preparing the consolidated balance-sheets shown in Table 39, figures were taken from the actual balance-sheet nearest to 31 March each year, and no attempt was made to adjust for differences in

[1] Bank of Scotland, 28 Feb.; British Linen Bank, 30 Sept.; Clydesdale and North of Scotland Bank, 31 Dec.; Commercial Bank of Scotland, variable but near end of Oct.; National Bank of Scotland, 1 Nov.; Royal Bank of Scotland, 10 Oct. to 1953, then 31 Dec.; and Union Bank of Scotland, 2 Apr. 1953 and 27th 1954.

TABLE 39

Clearing and Scottish banks consolidated balance-sheet

Liabilities	*1953*	*1954*	*1955*	*Assets*	*1953*	*1954*	*1955*
	£ m.				£ m.		
1. Capital and reserves	189	197	206	4. Cash	559	550	577
2. Deposits (net)	6,636	6,848	7,042	5. Money at call and short notice	604	569	568
3. Liabilities to subsidiaries (net)	38	38	37	6. Treasury bills	1,207	1,353	1,210
				7. Other bills	71	87	128
				8. Investments:			
				(*a*) British government and guaranteed	2,397	2,553	2,628
				(*b*) Dominion, colonial, and local authority	44	58	68
				(*c*) Other investments	26	19	21
				9. Subsidiaries and trade investments	35	35	33
				10. Advances	1,848	1,789	1,980
				11. Premises and other property	53	54	56
				12. Balances abroad	11	11	11
				13. Other assets	7	5	5
Total	6,863	7,083	7,285	Total	6,863	7,083	7,285

timing. A number of other adjustments were made, however, and some others should be made but cannot for lack of information. Both categories are briefly described in the following paragraphs.

The National Bank, which is one of the London clearing banks, does most of its business in Ireland and, as it was not possible to separate the English and Irish business, this bank has been left out of the table. The bank accounts for only about 1½ per cent. of all clearing-bank business. Lloyds Bank has some business in India, which is included in its ordinary balance-sheet, and for which it was not possible to make any allowance.

Where one bank is a subsidiary of another the parent company's holding has been omitted from 'Capital and reserves' on the liabilities side and from 'Subsidiaries and trade investments' on the assets side of the balance-sheet. The holdings concerned are those of Lloyds in the National Bank of Scotland, the National Provincial in Coutts, and the Royal Bank of Scotland in Glyn Mills and Williams Deacons'.

Gross deposits include items in course of collection, balances with other banks, and items in transit between branches of the same bank. All banks show items in course of collection and balances with other banks separately, and it is customary to deduct these from gross deposits in order to reach a figure for net deposits, a custom which we have followed. There is some discrepancy between the banks in their treatment of items in transit between branches. Lloyds is the only one to show them separately; the National Provincial and Coutts apparently include them with items in course of collection and balances with other banks. All the rest include them with 'Advances to customers and other accounts', so that both deposits and advances would be artificially inflated. We have, therefore, estimated the amount of items in transit for banks other than the National Provincial and Coutts, on the assumption that they bear the same proportion to deposits as do those of Lloyds, and have deducted this from deposits and also from advances. Both the deposits and advances categories, however, still contain some internal accounts including pension funds and provision for depreciation of investments, but, on the basis of information at present published, it is impossible to eliminate these.

Besides the instances already mentioned in which one clearing bank controls another, the banks have various subsidiary companies and interests in other companies. Some of these are very small, and have little or no economic significance, e.g. nominee companies and Channel Island executor and trustee companies. In other cases, the subsidiaries are important, though operating outside the group at present under consideration, e.g. Barclays Bank, Dominion, Colonial and Overseas, and Lloyds and National Provincial Foreign Bank. The capital of all these is entered at book value. Treatment of minority interests, e.g. the banks' holdings in the Industrial and Commercial Finance Corporation, follows the same lines.

Thus, the item 'Subsidiaries and trade investments' includes all these interests except the holding of the parent company in another clearing or Scottish bank. Current balances due to and from subsidiaries have been offset against one another, and the result is a net item, 'Liabilities to subsidiaries', which represents the net liability of all banks in the group to subsidiaries outside it.

Under the Currency and Banknotes Act, 1928, the Scottish banks are given an 'authorized circulation' of notes, amounting to £2,676,350, and are required to hold backing for all notes in excess of this in gold or silver coin or Bank of England notes. This holding is, of course, shown as 'Cash' in the balance-sheets. In order to avoid duplication in the combined account, however, only the authorized circulation of Scottish notes has been included on the liabilities side and cash held as backing for the note issue has been deducted from the assets side of the balance-sheet. The amount of these Scottish notes was £85 m. in 1953, £92 m. in 1954, and £98 m. in 1955.

The banks' cash is divided roughly equally between balances with the Bank of England and notes and coin. An exact statement is impossible because of differences in timing. The Bank of England return which gives bankers' balances (though for a rather wider group than the clearing and Scottish banks) is published each Wednesday; the clearing-bank returns refer to the third Wednesday of each month except June and December, when they are made up on the last day of the month; the official returns of currency circulation refer to the average of Wednesdays for Bank of England notes and coin held by the clearing banks and to the average of Saturdays for notes and coin held by the Scottish banks. The figures are as follows:

£ m. December

	1952	*1953*	*1954*
1. Cash (balance-sheet total) . . .	559·0	549·8	577·3
2. Plus backing for Scottish notes .	83·0	89·5	95·3
	642·0	639·3	672·6
3. Less notes and coin	315·2	334·5	362·7
4. Balance	326·8	304·8	309·9
5. Bank of England ('Bankers' balances')	302·8 (31 Dec. 1952)	290·2 (30 Dec. 1953)	276·1 (30 Dec. 1954)

There are two possible reasons why the balance shown in line 4 exceeds the figure for bankers' deposits at the Bank of England. The banks' holding of notes and coin probably rises somewhat at the end of the month as shopkeepers pay in their Christmas takings. Also, the Bank of England return is not for 31 December apart from 1952 and the banks arrange their transactions so that there is a substantial increase in their balances at the Bank during the last day or two of the year.

'Money at call and short notice' consists mainly of loans to the Discount Market together with some loans to the Stock Exchange. There is no published division between the two since the Second World War. The financial crisis of August 1914 revealed that the London Stock Exchange had loans of £81 m. and provincial exchanges of £11 m. outstanding, rather less than half from clearing banks.[1] The Macmillan Committee published a break-down for the clearing banks and the Scottish banks from 1919 to 1930, which showed clearing-bank loans to

[1] E. V. Morgan, *Studies on British Financial Policy, 1914–25*, Macmillan, London, 1952, p. 26.

TABLE 40

Five merchant banks: Hambros, Baring Bros., Erlangers, Blydenstein, and S. Japhet & Co. combined balance-sheet

Liabilities	1953 (£ m.)	1954 (£ m.)	1955 (£ m.)	*Assets*	1953 (£ m.)	1954 (£ m.)	1955 (£ m.)
1. Capital and reserves	12·2	12·5	13·3	3. Cash	7·1	7·4	7·3
2. Deposits	70·1	76·5	88·4	4. Call-money	23·7	23·0	28·2
				5. Bills	11·5	13·4	16·5
				6. Investments:			
				(*a*) British government and guaranteed	15·6	16·9	18·0
				(*b*) Other	6·9	7·2	7·4
				7. Advances	17·3	20·6	22·9
				8. Other assets	0·2	0·5	0·7
Total	82·3	89·0	100·7	Total	82·3	89·0	100·7

the Stock Exchange varying in annual average from about £20 m. in the early post-war years to £48 m. in 1928, and falling again to £28 m. in 1930. The Scottish bank loans were much smaller ranging from a few hundred thousand to about 1¾ m.[1] It is believed that these loans rose again during the 1930's, possibly to about £50 m.[2] The Second World War had a profound effect on the Stock Exchange in several ways. There has, of course, been a vast increase in the value of quoted securities, especially gilt-edged. On the other hand, the number and resources of the jobbers has not increased to anything like the same extent, and the jobbing function in short-dated gilt-edged has largely passed to the discount houses. Moreover, the amount of speculative dealing has declined. On balance, it would be surprising if short loans to the Stock Exchange amounted to much more than the £50 m. of pre-war years.

About 95 per cent. of the banks' investments are in government and government guaranteed securities. This category includes nationalization issues, but the banks' holding of these is not likely to be very large because of their long redemption date. There are no published statistics of the composition, by date, of bank investments but in recent years bank chairmen have been at pains to assure shareholders in their annual speeches of the high proportion of short-dated stocks in their portfolios. The leader in this movement was the Midland. In January 1954 Lord Harlech stated: 'At the same time, we have strengthened still further the safeguards against capital depreciation of our investments in British government securities. To-day, more than half the total have final maturity dates within the next five years, and nine-tenths, within ten years'.[3] The following year he said that 'all of them bear final maturity dates falling within the next eleven years'.[4] Other banks were rather slower to volunteer information and somewhat less precise. A typical statement of a kind that is now made annually almost as a matter of course is: 'We hold no undated government securities, and the majority

[1] Report of Committee on Finance and Industry, Cmd. 3897, 1931, pp. 284 sqq.
[2] T. Balogh, *Studies in Financial Organisation*, Cambridge, 1947, pp. 59–60.
[3] *The Economist*, 23 Jan. 1954, p. 285.
[4] Ibid., 29 Jan. 1955.

TABLE 41

Other non-clearing banks' combined balance-sheet

Liabilities	1953 (£ m.)	1954	1955	Assets	1953 (£ m.)	1954	1955
1. Capital and reserves	18·0	18·8	19·9	4. Cash[1]	30·6	32·4	32·6
2. Deposits (net)	414·2	423·5	439·4	5. Call-money[2]	61·9	57·4	60·8
3. Creditors, &c.	0·3	0·3	0·3	6. Bills[3]	6·3	6·9	9·1
				7. Investments:			
				(a) Government securities	220·7	214·1	211·8
				(b) Local authorities	34·9	47·6	57·8
				(c) Overseas quoted	9·6	10·7	12·7
				(d) Other quoted	4·2	3·3	3·3
				(e) Unquoted	0·1	0·2	0·1
				8. Advances	59·1	64·6	66·1
				9. Premises	2·3	2·4	2·4
				10. Other assets	2·8	3·1	2·4
Total	432·5	442·6	459·6	Total	432·5	442·6	459·6

[1] In the case of Yorkshire Penny Bank, probably includes call-money.

[2] Includes deposits of Birmingham Municipal Bank with Birmingham Corporation and 'other liquid funds' of the C.W.S. banks, some of which may be in bills.

[3] Includes small sums deposited by the Birmingham Municipal Bank with the National Debt Commissioners in 1953 and 1954.

of our holdings mature within ten years.' (Mr. D. J. Robarts, National Provincial, Jan. 1956.)[1]

The item described as 'advances to customers and other accounts' contains some internal items, including pension funds, which it is impossible to eliminate. The clearing banks do not publish an analysis of their advances, but the British Bankers' Association publishes an analysis for all its members at quarterly intervals, in February, May, August, and November. The analysis is by industry or occupation, but it also gives some clue to the sector which is borrowing. The figures, in annual averages, are as follows:

£ *m.*

	1953	*1954*	*1955*
Mainly company sector (Manufacturing, industry, shipping and shipbuilding, entertainment)	528	520	581
Company and personal sectors (Building and contracting retail trade, unclassified industry and trade)	338	351	400
Company and public sectors (Transport and communications)	18	18	21
Mainly personal sector (Personal and professional agriculture stockbrokers)	573	601	635
Public sector (Mining utilities, other than transport, local authorities)	167	211	255
Financial	179	193	216
Charities	13	13	14
Total	1,816	1,908	2,120

B. MERCHANT BANKS

The merchant banks have a great variety of functions, mainly concerned with the finance of international trade, and with the launching of new security issues, though they also accept deposits from the public and make loans to customers. Most of them are private companies and do not publish accounts. An aggregate balance-sheet summary for five firms whose accounts are available is shown in Table 40. The firms in this table account for just under a quarter of the paid-up capital of the

[1] *The Economist*, 21 Jan. 1956, p. 250.

group.[1] In compiling the consolidated statement of Tables 43 and 44 we have, therefore, multiplied the figures of Table 40 by four. The result is, however, only a very rough estimate, as there is a great deal of variety among the different firms, and it is by no means certain that the few which publish accounts are typical.[2]

C. OTHER BANKS

The other banks whose balance-sheets are summarized in Table 41 comprise two West End banks (Grindlays and C. Hoare & Co.), the Co-operative Wholesale Society Bank, and the Scottish Co-operative Wholesale Society Bank; the Birmingham Municipal Bank, the Isle of Man Bank, and the Yorkshire Penny Bank. Again, there is a considerable variety in the type of business undertaken. The Birmingham Municipal Bank is in many ways more like a savings bank than an ordinary commercial bank, with the bulk of its funds employed either in government securities or in loans to the corporation. All the banks concerned receive deposits from the general public, but nearly half of those of the C.W.S. banks come from the trading departments of the movement.

The accounting conventions of these banks are less standardized than those of the clearing banks. The Yorkshire Penny Bank does not show 'call-money' as a separate item, and the C.W.S. banks have an item 'other liquid funds' which comes immediately after 'cash' in the balance-sheet, and which presumably includes both call-money and bills. Thus, while the first three items of Table 41 together give a true picture of the liquid assets of the group, the individual items are not very accurate.

D. THE DISCOUNT HOUSES

The discount market consisted at this time of twelve firms: three large and old-established public companies; seven smaller

[1] Cf. N. Macrae, *The London Capital Market*, London, 1955, pp. 77–79. Macrae gives the total capital of the fifteen members of the Accepting Houses Committee as 'over £30 million'. The capital, excluding reserves, of the five firms in Table 40 was £8 m.

[2] The Report of the Committee on the Working of the Monetary System (Radcliffe Report), London, 1959, para. 186, gives figures for 1958 which suggest that our estimate is rather too high.

TABLE 42

The discount houses' estimated assets and liabilities

Liabilities	*1953* (£ m.)	*1954* (£ m.)	*1955* (£ m.)	*Assets*	*1953* (£ m.)	*1954* (£ m.)	*1955* (£ m.)
1. Capital and reserves	32	34	35	4. Cash	11	12	12
2. Loans	1,050	1,070	1,100	5. Bills:			
3. Deposits	28	26	35	(*a*) Treasury	715	630	630
				(*b*) Other	65	80	110
				6. Investments	312	390	397
				7. Advances and debtors	7	18	21
Total	1,110	1,130	1,170	Total	1,110	1,130	1,170

TABLE 43

Combined statement of assets and liabilities of the banking system

Liabilities	1953	1954	1955	Assets	1953	1954	1955
	£ m.				£ m.		
1. Capital and reserves	288	300	314	5. Cash:[3]			
2. Deposits[1]	7,347	7,592	7,854	(a) With Bank of England	290	276	245
3. Loans from outside the system[2]	378	441	445	(b) Notes and coin	328	336	394
4. Net liability to subsidiaries	38	38	37	6. Call-money, &c., lent outside system[4]	89	89	87
				7. Treasury bills	1,922	1,983	1,840
				8. Other bills	188	228	313
				9. Investments:			
				(a) Government and government guaranteed	2,992	3,225	3,309
				(b) Other	147	168	193
				10. Subsidiaries and trade investments	35	35	33
				11. Advances	1,983	1,954	2,159
				12. Premises	55	56	58
				13. Balances abroad	11	11	11
				14. Other assets	11	10	10
Total	8,051	8,371	8,651	Total	8,051	8,371	8,651

[1] Less cash held by discount houses.

[2] Loans by discount market less proportion of call-money of other banks assumed to go to discount market.

[3] Cash held by all institutions except discount houses. Bankers' balances taken at end-year.

[4] Other than that lent to discount market, i.e. £50 m., assumed to be lent to Stock Exchange and Birmingham Municipal Bank deposits with Corporation.

public companies, mostly formed out of old private firms,[1] one very new private company, and one old-established private firm which acts as broker to the Bank of England.

The traditional business of the market is the discounting of bills of exchange, though the Treasury bill now far exceeds the commercial bill in importance. Unlike the clearing banks, the discount houses do not distinguish between Treasury bills and other bills in their balance-sheets. They do, however, show in footnotes their contingent liability in respect of bills rediscounted. These liabilities were:

	£ m.	
1953	*1954*	*1955*
57·0	71·9	97·6

Commercial bills are usually resold to the banks when they have run for between half and two-thirds of their life,[2] so that actual holdings at the time of the balance-sheet are probably rather greater than rediscounts. This is the basis of the very rough estimate in Table 42.

A relatively new activity of the market is dealing in short-dated government bonds. This originated in the nineteen-thirties and assumed substantial proportions during and immediately after the Second World War. The securities concerned are normally within five years of maturity.

Besides using their own capital and reserves, the discount houses also accept deposits, though the amount involved is comparatively small. Their main source of funds is loans at call or short notice from the clearing banks, other British banks including the merchant banks, and from banks operating overseas.

Table 42 is compiled from the published balance-sheets of the public companies with an allowance for private companies based on Mr. W. T. C. King's estimate in his annual article in *The Banker*. The table, however, gives only a very approximate picture, as the balance-sheets are made up on different dates[3]

[1] One of these, Ryders, became a public company only in 1954.

[2] W. T. C. King in *The Banker*, Aug. 1951, p. 97.

[3] Alexanders' the National and the Union on 31 Dec.; Gillett Bros., Jessel, Toynbee & Co., and Smith, St. Aubyn & Co. on 31 Mar.; Allen, Harvey & Ross, and Cater, Brightewn & Co. on 5 Apr.; King & Shaxson on 30 Apr., and Ryders on 31 May.

and there is a very strong seasonal variation in the discount markets' holding of Treasury bills associated with the fluctuations in government revenue and expenditure. The fact that the three largest houses make up their accounts on 31 December, when the Treasury bill issue is at its seasonal peak, tends to exaggerate both the bill portfolio and the borrowing of the market. The problem of adjusting for this, both for the banks and the discount market, is discussed in the succeeding paragraphs.

Table 43 presents a consolidated statement for the banking system, including the discount market, as a whole, which is made up from Tables 39 to 42, eliminating items which occur in more than one. Further adjustment is, however, necessary in order to make the figures reasonably comparable with those of other sectors. As already noted, there is a strong seasonal movement in the Treasury bill issue, which is associated with changes in the bill portfolio and borrowings of the discount houses, and with variations in the banks' holding of bills and call-money, and in their deposits. There is also an element of seasonal variation in the advances of the banks and these seasonal changes, together with other longer-term economic forces, may involve changes also in cash and, possibly, in investments.

Adjustment for the clearing banks is comparatively easy. In Table 44 we have simply substituted the March clearing bank figures for the December ones. These refer to the third Wednesday of the month whereas the statistics of the national debt in Chapter 2 relate to 31 March, but this does not matter greatly; the seasonal revenue influx is nearly over by the middle of March and there is normally little change in the debt during the second half of the month. For Scottish and other non-clearing banks, the spread of accounting dates reduces the distortion involved. The only possible method of adjusting their figures would be to assume that they followed the same seasonal pattern as the clearing banks; in view of the big differences in their business, however, it seems unlikely that this would give any better picture than the crude figures, and no adjustment has been made.

There remains the problem of the discount market, which is

TABLE 44

Estimated assets and liabilities of the banking system, 31 March 1952–5

Liabilities	*1953* (£ m.)	*1954* (£ m.)	*1955* (£ m.)	*Assets*	*1953* (£ m.)	*1954* (£ m.)	*1955* (£ m.)
1. Capital and reserves	288	300	314	5. Cash:			
2. Deposits	7,011	7,347	7,389	(*a*) With Bank of England	269	263	276
3. Discount market loans from outside system	373	432	429	(*b*) Notes and coin	297	319	306
4. Net liabilities to subsidiaries	38	38	37	6. Call-money lent outside system	89	89	87
				7. Treasury bills	1,618	1,698	1,414
				8. Other bills	191	232	315
				9. Investments:			
				(*a*) Government and guaranteed	2,966	3,219	3,237
				(*b*) Other	147	168	193
				10. Subsidiaries and trade investments	35	36	33
				11. Advances	2,021	2,017	2,231
				12. Premises	55	56	58
				13. Balances abroad	11	11	11
				14. Other assets	11	10	10
Total	7,710	8,117	8,170	Total	7,710	8,117	8,170

very difficult as the seasonal pattern was disturbed each year by special influences. In 1952–3 and 1953–4 the supply of bills at the end-year peak was reduced by the surrender of bills by way of cash subscription to new issues of stock, and in the spring of 1955 the movement of relative interest rates was such as to cause an exceptional demand for bills from non-banking sources. In Table 44 we have assumed that the bill portfolio of the discount market declined in the same proportion as the clearing banks' call-money, but this may well be very wide of the mark.

The position may be briefly summarized, using the March 1955 figures. At that date the banking system had a total capital and reserves of £314 m. It received £7,450 m. of deposits and, in addition, the discount market borrowed around £430 m. in short loans from outside sources. On the assets side, the system held about £1,500 m. of Treasury bills, just under half the total tender bill issue (though this proportion, for reasons already mentioned, was unusually low). Of these, very roughly £560 m. would be held by the discount market and the remainder by the banks.

The system also held nearly £3,300 m. of government securities,[1] about 22 per cent. of the quoted national debt, and nearly £2,300 m. of advances.

There is one very important omission, in the group of banks, both British and foreign owned, whose business is mainly overseas. Some of these banks receive deposits from British customers and a few of them even operate current accounts for them. They all keep balances in London, which they employ largely in the money market, and some of them hold substantial amounts of Treasury bills and other government securities. The Radcliffe Committee collected information from 55 of them out of a total of about 75. In February 1959 these had sterling assets of over £1,055 m., and sterling deposits of £922 m., of which more than £700 m. were on account of non-residents.[2]

[1] This figure includes a certain amount of nationalization stocks, but the amount is likely to be fairly small, as the stocks concerned were far too long for the discount market, and longer than the clearing banks normally like.

[2] Committee on the working of the Monetary System, Report. Cmd. 827, 1959, paras. 197–201.

9

NON-BANKING FINANCIAL INSTITUTIONS

WE include in this chapter all financial companies not engaged in banking: insurance companies, investment trusts, hire-purchase finance houses, property companies, and three large semi-official institutions—the Industrial and Commercial Finance Corporation, the Agricultural Mortgage Corporation, and the Finance Corporation for Industry. Also included here are pension funds (which are occasionally registered as companies but usually not), building societies, and the Special Investment Department of the Trustee savings banks.

A. INSURANCE COMPANIES

Insurance companies furnish fairly comprehensive returns to the Board of Trade, which form the basis of Table 45. The main problems which arise in incorporating the figures into our present analysis concern the treatment of foreign business and the method of valuation.

Companies established in Great Britain do about 9 per cent. of their life business, measured by premium income, abroad; an appreciable, though unknown, proportion of general insurance business is also on foreign account. Companies established outside Great Britain, which undertake British business, also furnish balance-sheets to the Board of Trade, but their usefulness for our present purpose is limited because they do not separate Britain and overseas business. Premiums received for life assurance, however, amounted to rather less than half those received by British companies for foreign business, and amounted to about 4 per cent. of all life premiums. Table 45 takes account only of companies established in Great Britain, and the known British assets and liabilities of overseas insurance companies are discussed in Chapter 11.

TABLE 45

Insurance companies (life and other) established within Great Britain. Combined balance-sheet

Liabilities (£ m.)	*1953*	*1954*	*1955*	*Assets* (£ m.)	*1953*	*1954*	*1955*
1. Capital and reserves	302	319	363	5. British government securities	760	758	766
2. Insurance funds:				6. Government guaranteed securities	385	454	481
(*a*) Life	2,661	2,865	3,113	7. Local authority securities	99	99	102
(*b*) Other	432	454	465	8. Overseas government and municipal	369	386	402
3. Outstanding claims	206	220	247	9. Debentures	411	464	543
4. Outstanding accounts, creditors, &c.	209	229	249	10. Preference, and guaranteed stocks and shares	264	279	312
				11. Ordinary stocks and shares	456	507	619
				12. Mortgages	362	396	430
				13. Loans on policies	42	46	49
				14. Land and property	257	286	312
				15. Agents balances	252	260	279
				16. Cash	144	141	131
				17. Other assets	8	11	11
Total	3,809	4,087	4,437	Total	3,809	4,087	4,437

Source: Board of Trade.

The value placed on a number of items in balance-sheets differs from the basis of valuation which we have used. Securities are normally valued at cost. Those which depreciate in value may be written down, and those which appreciate are occasionally written up, though this appears to be rare. The result is probably to undervalue securities as a whole, especially ordinary shares. No adjustment is made for this here, though a guess is made in Chapter 12.

A further problem arises as to the sectors to which insurance-company liabilities should be attributed as assets. The National Income Blue Book treats the annual increase in life-assurance funds as part of personal saving, and we follow the same principle in regarding life-assurance funds (less the small proportion in respect of foreign business) as 'belonging' to the personal sector. This accords with common sense, as a life policy is a very personal thing which is certainly regarded as an asset by its holder and which can be used as security for a loan. With other forms of insurance, the position is different. A fire or accident policy, for example, is not regarded as an asset by its holder and the reserves held against such policies cannot be attributed to any particular policy-holder or even to any particular sector. We have, therefore, placed them in the 'unallocated' column in the general table of Chapter 12.

B. PENSION FUNDS

The pension fund movement has been growing very rapidly in recent years; the annual increase in funds is a major constituent of personal saving, and the funds themselves have now reached a size where they are an important influence on the capital market.

The general principle we have followed in dealing with pension funds is to take account, so far as possible, of all funded schemes, and to assess the value of accumulated pension rights by the assets held in the funds. Unfunded schemes even though contributory, as in the case of civil servants and teachers, are not included, and neither are actuarial deficiencies in funded schemes.

The superannuation schemes of local authorities have been covered in Chapter 4, and certain schemes in the nationalized industries where the fund was merely left on deposit with the corporation, in Chapter 3. Co-operative societies have funded schemes, but practically all their assets are invested within the movement, and they are, therefore, included in Chapter 7. Some funds, especially those of the smaller private firms, are held in various forms of life-assurance policy and these have been included with the other business of the insurance companies. We are now concerned with funded schemes, whose funds are independently invested, both in the nationalized industries and in the private sector.

The Phillips Committee[1] published figures, compiled by the Institute of Actuaries and the Faculty of Actuaries in Scotland, relating to about 2,100 privately administered schemes, other than those of local authorities. No precise date is given for these figures, but they may be presumed to refer to 1953. The funds concerned had total assets at book values of approximately £1,000 m. and were growing at about £115 m. a year. Approximately £100 m. of this sum is represented by Transport and Gas funds held on deposit with the respective corporations and discussed in Chapter 3.

Unfortunately, the Phillips Committee gave no breakdown of pension-fund assets and, as practically no information on this point was available, a special inquiry was carried out. With the co-operation of the Association of Superannuation and Pension Funds, a questionnaire was sent to all their members except those known to have life-office schemes. Funds were asked for the value of their assets, at their balance-sheet date in 1953 and 1955, subdivided into the various categories set out in Table 46. Excluding co-operative societies and local authorities, and a few replies which were not sufficiently detailed to be useful, we obtained information about 359 funds, with total assets of £397 m. in 1953 and £546 m. in 1955. So far as we could tell, the sample was fairly representative of the whole field in the pro-

[1] *Report of the Committee on the Economic and Financial Problems of the Provision for Old Age*, Cmd. 9333, H.M.S.O., 1954, appendix v.

portion of large and small funds which it included, but it was not entirely representative in its coverage—in particular, the banks maintained their customary reserve, so that their funds are heavily under represented. About 25 per cent. of all funds (by asset value) gave figures at book value and the remainder at market value; no adjustment has been made for this in Table 46. A few funds lumped together two or more categories, and in

TABLE 46

The assets of pension funds

(*as shown by sample inquiry*)

£ *m.*

	1953	*1955*
1. British government and guaranteed securities	173·2	198·9
2. Overseas government, &c., securities	19·1	25·8
3. Local authorities and public boards	31·3	38·2
4. Debentures	42·6	62·6
5. Preference shares	31·6	37·6
6. Ordinary shares	64·5	133·5
7. Mortgages	15·2	18·9
8. Real Property	6·7	11·1
9. Other investments	6·3	9·7
10. Cash	7·1	10·1
Total	397·6	546·4

these cases the combined figure was distributed in the same proportion as held for other funds.

The Phillips Committee admits that its figures are not complete, but the understatement of assets is not likely to be large. A high proportion of the total assets of pension funds is held by a moderate number of large funds while, at the other end of the scale, a large number of very small funds make only a modest contribution to the total assets. In our sample 32 per cent. of all funds, with assets of over £1 m. each, held 89 per cent. of all assets, while 56 per cent. of the funds, of less than £500,000 each, held only 5 per cent. of the total. While a considerable number of the tiny funds may have escaped the notice of the actuaries reporting to the Institute, the coverage of the larger funds is likely to have been very thorough.

In 1953 some, though certainly not all, of the funds' ordinary shares would have had a market value higher than their book value; on the other hand, most of their gilt-edged stock would have shown a quite heavy depreciation. It is unlikely, therefore, that total assets had a market value much, if any, above their book value. Between mid-1953 and mid-1955 ordinary share prices rose substantially, while gilt-edged fell slightly. Those of our funds that made returns in market values, showed a growth between 1953 and 1955 of £46 m. a year; if they had added to their assets only their share of the new money coming into the movement (as shown by the Phillips Report) they would have grown at £35 m. a year. However, the sample included several large, fairly new, and very rapidly growing funds, so there may well have been some upward bias in the rate of growth, apart from the question of valuation. It would appear, therefore, that different methods of valuation have only a slight effect on the estimate of total assets, though they would, of course, have a larger one on estimates of the relative importance of different types of asset. Our sample appears to cover approximately 40 per cent. of all the funds with which we are concerned and, in compiling Table 52, the figures of Table 46 have been multiplied by 2·5.

C. HIRE-PURCHASE FINANCE COMPANIES

The subject of hire-purchase finance has been something of a mystery until very recently. Since the end of 1955, however, the Board of Trade has published estimates of total hire-purchase debt, and a recent study[1] has added considerably to our knowledge of the operations of the hire-purchase finance houses. There is still, however, no precise and comprehensive information and much of that which we have relates only to a time later than 1953–5.

The Board of Trade estimated that, at the end of 1955, hire-purchase debt amounted to at least £450 m., of which £281 m. was owing to retailers and £169 m. to finance houses. The sums owing to retailers represent credit given by them out of their

[1] *Hire-Purchase in a Free Society*, edited by Ralph Harris and Arthur Seldon. Institute of Economic Affairs, London, 1958.

own resources, out of bank loans, or out of trade credit which they have, themselves, received from suppliers. In our analysis, therefore, it is a liability of the personal sector to the company sector. It is the credit given by specialist finance houses with which we are concerned here.

At the end of 1955 finance houses accounted for 37 per cent. of total hire-purchase debt. Since then the proportion has varied between 38 and 50 per cent. but it has usually been just over 40 per cent. There are a few large firms and a great many very small ones engaged in the business and there has been a big increase in the number of small houses in recent years. Most of the larger firms are members of the Finance Houses Association and, between June 1956 and December 1957, the eleven members of the Association did between 70 and 84 per cent. of all finance-house business.[1] Apart from a sharp drop at the end of 1956, there was a tendency for the share of F.H.A. members to increase, in spite of the growing number of small firms in the field.

There are a number of sources from which the finance houses raise their funds: their own capital and reserves; bank overdrafts; the drawing of bills which are accepted by one of the accepting houses and then discounted; and the receiving of loans and deposits from the public. The balance-sheets are not compiled in a way which enables each of these items to be separated, but an analysis of the accounts of ten of the eleven members of the F.H.A. for the years 1954–5 to 1956–7 showed that capital and reserves (including 'deferred income') provided 36 per cent. of total resources; deposits 34 per cent. and bank loans and acceptances 30 per cent.[2] The emergence of the clearing banks as shareholders in finance houses is after the end of our period. It is known, however, that several insurance companies and at least one pension fund held shares, but it has not been possible to estimate the amount of these holdings.

About 90 per cent. of the total assets of the larger finance houses are employed in hire-purchase loans, about 3½ per cent.

[1] Harris and Seldon, op. cit., p 12. A twelfth firm joined the F.H.A. in the summer of 1957.

[2] Ibid., p. 37.

in liquid assets, and about $6\frac{1}{2}$ per cent. in other assets. There is no direct evidence on the distribution of credit between companies and persons, but an analysis of the proportion of loans in respect of different types of goods gives a fair idea. In December 1955 these proportions were:

	%
Goods bought mainly by persons	
Cars (new and second-hand) and motor-cycles	50
Radio and television	8
Farm equipment	3
Furniture and domestic appliances	5
Caravans	2
Miscellaneous	5
	73
Bought mainly by companies	
Commercial vehicles	20
Industrial plant	7
	100

In compiling Table 47 we have assumed that members of the Finance Houses Association did 70 per cent. of all finance-house business, that they derived their resources in the same way as in the average of 1955–7; that 90 per cent. of total resources were employed in hire-purchase; and that 75 per cent. of hire-purchase loans were to the personal sector.

TABLE 47

Estimated assets and liabilities of hire-purchase finance companies

Liabilities (£ m.)	*1953*	*1954*	*1955*	*Assets* (£ m.)	*1953*	*1954*	*1955*
1. Capital and reserves	38	52	81	4. Hirers' balances	95	130	203
2. Deposits	36	50	77	5. Liquid assets	4	6	8
3. Bank loans and bills	32	44	68	6. Other assets	7	10	15
Total	106	146	226	Total	106	146	226

D. BUILDING SOCIETIES

The building societies are another group which has been growing very rapidly in recent years. There are nearly 800 societies but 130 of them with assets of over £1 m. do nearly 80 per cent. of all business. Their business is, of course, primarily the finance of house purchase and nearly 85 per cent. of their assets are employed in this way. The balance is held in cash, in government securities, and in loans to local authorities. The societies derive their funds from the public through either deposits or shares. The 'shares' are very different from most other form of share; they carry a guaranteed rate of interest, which is varied from time to time; they are not marketable, but they can be withdrawn at their full face value subject to a period of notice. They are thus more like savings certificates than any other form of security. Shares are held almost exclusively by persons, though

TABLE 48

Assets and liabilities of building societies

Liabilities	*1953* (£ m.)	*1954* (£ m.)	*1955* (£ m.)	*Assets*	*1953* (£ m.)	*1954* (£ m.)	*1955* (£ m.)
1. Shares . .	1,339	1,537	1,732	6. Mortgages .	1,396	1,574	1,752
2. Deposits . .	202	220	217	7. Investments:			
3. Bank loans .	2	2	2	(*a*) quoted .	92	110	120
4. Other liabilities	16	19	19	(*b*) unquoted .	92	110	120
5. Reserves . .	84	90	96	8. Cash . .	49	58	59
				9. Other assets .	12	13	14
Total . .	1,643	1,867	2,066	Total . .	1,643	1,867	2,066

we have come across a few small holdings by charities. Deposits are also mainly personal, though some companies deposit fairly large sums.

The societies submit returns to the Chief Registrar of Friendly Societies, which are summarized in his annual report, and a rather fuller summary of balance-sheets for societies which are members of the Building Societies Association (which almost all the big ones are) appears in the *Building Societies Yearbook*. Table 48 is based on the reports of the Chief Registrar supplemented by the analysis of balance-sheets of the 130 societies with assets over £1 m.

E. INVESTMENT TRUSTS

Though there is considerable variety among them, the essence of the investment trust is, of course, that the investor should be able to spread his risks by participating indirectly in a large number of undertakings while, at the same time, securing the benefits of expert investment management. These benefits naturally appeal mainly to the personal investor of comparatively modest resources.

Our main source of information has been the analysis of balance-sheets contained in the *Stock Exchange Yearbook*. The 1955 analysis, referring to balance-sheets of various dates in 1954, covers 264 quoted trusts with a capital of £423 m. and with investments of a book value of £527 m. and a market value of £744 m. It was possible to separate British and overseas investments for trusts with a market value of £690 m. and, assuming the same proportions held for the rest, the total portfolio would comprise:

	£ m.	%
British securities .	428	58
Overseas securities .	316	42

Trusts with a portfolio of £701 m. provided a split between debentures, preference, and ordinary shares, from which we estimate the following totals:

	£ m.	%
Debentures . .	83	11
Preference shares .	92	12
Ordinary shares .	569	77

Unfortunately it was not possible to analyse British and foreign holdings separately by type of share, and the estimates in Table 49 are based on the rather risky assumption that the same proportion held for both.

Besides the trusts covered in the *Stock Exchange Yearbook* analysis, there are some which are quoted only on provincial exchanges, for which we had no information.

Unit trusts (whose funds are invested, in fixed or variable proportions, in a given list of ordinary shares) held about £100 m. in 1953.[1] Allowing for the rise in share prices between 1953 and 1955, they probably held about £140 m. in 1954 and £180 m. in 1955. These amounts are included in Table 52.

[1] N. Macrae, *The London Capital Market*, p. 85.

F. FINANCE AND PROPERTY COMPANIES

This group comprises companies classified in the *Stock Exchange Yearbook* as 'Financial Trusts, Land and Property', except for hire-purchase finance houses and the Industrial and Commercial Finance Corporation, the Finance Corporation for Industry, and the Agricultural Mortgage Corporation, for

TABLE 49

Investment trusts quoted on the London Stock Exchange
Estimated assets and liabilities

Liabilities	*1953*	*1954*	*1955*	*Assets*	*1953*	*1954*	*1955*
	£ *m.*				£ *m.*		
1. Capital	388	423	461	3. British securities:			
2. Reserves and hidden reserves	172	321	543	(*a*) Debentures	43	48	45
				(*b*) Preference	47	53	50
				(*c*) Ordinary	235	327	487
				4. Foreign stocks	235	316	422
Total	560	744	1,004	Total	560	744	1,004

TABLE 50

Finance and property companies. Estimated assets and liabilities

Liabilities	*1953*	*1954*	*1955*	*Assets*	*1953*	*1954*	*1955*
	£ *m.*				£ *m.*		
1. Capital and reserves	173	185	209	5. Fixed assets	226	254	281
2. Mortgages	77	78	79	6. Investments	21	21	21
3. Current liabilities	23	36	40	7. Subsidiaries and trade investments	11	10	9
4. Other liabilities	39	39	40	8. Cash	9	3	4
				9. Other current assets	40	46	52
				10. Other assets	5	4	2
Total	312	338	369	Total	312	338	369

which separate figures are given. The group is a heterogeneous one, including some companies whose interests are mainly financial, and some which are holding companies controlling other non-financial companies. In the main, however, they are property companies, and some two-thirds of their total assets are in real estate. The estimates given in Table 50 are based on analysis of all balance-sheet summaries in the *Stock Exchange Yearbook* for accounting years ending in 1954 and a one-in-ten sample for 1953 and 1955.

G. TRUSTEE SAVINGS BANKS, SPECIAL INVESTMENT DEPARTMENTS

The trustees of individual banks may, at their discretion, accept deposits from customers with at least £50 in the Ordinary Department, and invest the funds so received in a range of stocks, which includes local authority, dominions, and colonial issues as well as those of the central government. Purchases and sales of stock have to be approved by the National Debt Commissioners, but the initiative in the purchase and sale of stock lies with the Trustees. This is why we have excluded the Special Investment Departments from the public sector.

£ m. at 20 Nov.

	1952	*1953*	*1954*
British government and guaranteed securities	43·9	42·1	45·4
Local authority stocks	1·4	4·3	8·8
Local authority mortgages	80·2	98·5	137·1
Cash	3·2	5·1	6·8
Other assets	2·3	2·5	3·4
Total	131·0	152·5	201·5

Interest on these deposits is paid at a rate varying with the yield on investments and, in recent years, it has been well above the 2½ per cent. offered on ordinary deposits. Hence, business has grown very rapidly in recent years, and total assets in the departments increased from £131 m. in November 1952 to £202 m. in November 1954. The composition of these assets is shown above. Government securities include some nationalization stocks and some non-market issues, for which separate figures were not available. 'Other assets' include small amounts of Northern Ireland and overseas stocks, interest accrued, and premises.

H. OTHER FINANCIAL INSTITUTIONS

There are a number of other financial institutions which do not fall into any of the categories we have discussed. They are mainly official and semi-official bodies concerned with providing capital for special purposes or for special classes of borrower. The three most important are the Agricultural Mortgage

Corporation, the Finance Corporation for Industry, and the Industrial and Commercial Finance Corporation, and the balance-sheets of these three are analysed in Table 51.

TABLE 51

The Agricultural Mortgage Corporation, the Finance Corporation for Industry, and the Industrial and Commercial Finance Corporation combined balance-sheet

Liabilities	1953	1954	1955	*Assets*	1953	1954	1955
	£ m.				£ m.		
1. Capital and reserves	28·3	30·7	31·8	4. Cash	1·2	1·0	0·8
2. Current liabilities	62·6	60·7	55·1	5. Treasury bills	2·0	1·7	0·4
3. Loans	29·2	29·0	28·9	6. Government securities	3·3	3·3	3·3
				7. Other investments	87·0	86·6	82·5
				8. Loans, advances and debtors	25·8	27·0	28·2
				9. Other assets	0·8	0·7	0·6
Total	120·1	120·4	115·8	Total	120·1	120·4	115·8

SUMMARY

Table 52 shows the total estimated assets and liabilities of non-banking financial institutions. These are derived by adding the items of Tables 45 to 51 and making an appropriate allowance for the unit trusts and for the special investment departments of the savings banks. This involves a certain amount of duplication, particularly in respect of insurance-company and pension-fund holdings in investment trusts, and pension-fund holdings in insurance companies, but it was not possible to eliminate these. It should also be noted that the assets of pension funds and investment trusts are taken at estimated market value, while those of other institutions are at book value. Table 52 thus gives only a rough idea of the importance of this group of financial intermediairies.

Both the absolute figures and the rate of growth are impressive. By 1955 the group as a whole had resources of nearly £10,000 m., of which major items were nearly £2,000 m. of capital and reserves, over £3,500 m. of insurance funds and

TABLE 52

Estimated assets and liabilities of all non-banking financial institutions

£ *m.*

Liabilities	*1953*	*1954*	*1955*
1. Capital and reserves	1,294	1,569	1,974
2. Insurance funds	3,093	3,319	3,578
3. Pension funds	944	1,182	1,366
4. Mortgages	77	78	79
5. Shares in building societies	1,339	1,537	1,732
6. Deposits:			
(*a*) Building societies	202	220	217
(*b*) H.P. finance companies	36	50	77
(*c*) Savings banks, special investment depts.	122	144	193
7. Other liabilities	619	679	749
Total	7,775	8,776	9,966

£ *m.*

Assets	*1953*	*1954*	*1955*
8. Government and guaranteed stocks	1,719	1,834	1,913
9. Local authorities	351	399	464
10. Overseas securities	652	758	888
11. Debentures	561	644	745
12. Preference shares	390	419	456
13. Ordinary shares	952	1,222	1,620
14. Mortgages and policy loans	1,838	2,059	2,278
15. H.P. balances	95	130	203
16. Fixed assets	500	562	621
17. Cash	228	236	235
18. Other assets	488	513	541
Total	7,775	8,776	9,966

£1,350 m. of pension funds, and nearly £2,000 m. of shares and deposits in building societies. Only some £600 m. of these resources were in fixed assets, rather more than half owned by property companies and most of the rest by insurance companies. The remainder was all in financial assets of one kind or another. Nearly £1,900 m. (equivalent to over £2,000 m. in nominal values) was in government securities and nationalization issues. About £200 m. was in local authority stock, and a further £120 m. was on loan to local authorities, largely from the building societies. Nearly £2,500 m. was owing by persons—mortgages from building societies and insurance companies, loans from insurance companies on the security of policies, hire-purchase balances, and loans to farmers by the Agricultural Mortgage Corporation. Some £2,800 m. was invested in British companies, though this figure is much affected by the differences in valuation already mentioned. If ordinary shares held by investment trusts and pension funds had been expressed at their nominal values the figure would, of course, have been much reduced; if ordinary shares held by insurance companies had been taken at market value, however, it would have been substantially increased. Finally, there is nearly £900 m. in overseas stocks and this understates the total overseas investment of the group. While insurance companies show their holdings of foreign government and corporation stocks separately, they do not split their holdings of company stocks and shares. No allowance is made for this here though a rough estimate is attempted in Chapter 12.

10

CHARITIES AND SIMILAR NON-PROFIT ORGANIZATIONS

CHARITIES are defined for income-tax purposes as corporate bodies existing for the relief of poverty, for educational or religious purposes, or 'for the general benefit of the community'. The following broad categories are included:

(i) Churches and religious organizations. Apart from the Church Commissioners these organizations do not publish accounts and are not under the supervision of any official body.

(ii) Educational institutions. In general, these come under the supervision of the Minister of Education, though the universities and certain schools are exempt.

(iii) Hospitals, which have been included in the central government sector, and with which we are not concerned here.

(iv) Other charities which, so far as they come under any official body, are the responsibility of the Charity Commissioners.

(v) Friendly societies, including trade unions, which make returns to the Chief Registrar of Friendly Societies.

The income of these bodies is exempt from tax and the Inland Revenue Reports give figures for exemptions in respect of income assessed for tax. The amounts were as follows:

£ *m.*

	1952–3	*1953–4*	*1954–5*
Schedule A (real property)	18·9	18·9	18·9
Schedule B (British and foreign government securities)	10·0	10·0	10·0
Schedule D (business earnings) . .	20·8	21·8	21·8
Total	49·7	50·7	50·7

Some Schedule D income may be derived from real property, as rents in excess of Schedule A assessments are assessed under

Schedule D. However, the whole amount of such assessment in 1953–4 was only £40 m., so the amount falling on charities must have been small.

Income from government securities is assessed under Schedule B only if tax is deducted at source. Dividends of less than £5 a year are normally paid in full, and the terms of issue of some stocks, including $3\frac{1}{2}$ per cent. War Loan which is very popular with charities, provide that all dividends are paid without deduction. Thus, a large part of the income of charities from government securities escapes assessment. Moreover, apart from Schedule A, income is normally not assessed if it can be shown beforehand that it is to be used for charitable purposes. The whole of the income on securities held by the Official Trustee of Charitable Funds, and an unknown amount of other income avoids assessment in this way. The figures are thus only useful in getting a lower limit to the total assets of the group and they are used for this purpose later.

CHURCHES

Churches are exempt from the provisions of the Charitable Trusts Acts which require the submission of accounts to the appropriate official body. However, the Church Commissioners publish an annual report and statement of accounts. This understates their assets in that real property acquired since 1948 is valued at cost less depreciation, but property transferred to the Commission from the former Ecclesiastical Commissioners and Queen Anne's Bounty, without payment, has no book value. The Commissioners have, however, kindly furnished us with a separate estimate of the value of their real property as well as some other information supplementing their accounts. In addition, there is a substantial amount of Church of England property held in diocesan funds and by the Central Board of Finance. We were able to obtain figures from the Central Board, and from about half the dioceses. We were not able to obtain information about property held by individual parishes but it is believed that parochial property, apart from that held on behalf of parishes in diocesan funds, is fairly small.

The other religious denominations have much less property than the Church of England, but the aggregate is quite substantial. The central bodies of ten denominations were kind enough to send us information.[1] There were, however, several important denominations for which we were unable to obtain

TABLE 53

Estimated assets of churches

£ m.

	1953	*1954*	*1955*
1. British government securities:			
(*a*) Quoted	75	72	69
(*b*) Other	5	4	4
2. Government guaranteed securities	45	41	39
3. Local authorities and public boards	23	20	20
4. Overseas securities	8	6	5
5. Debentures and preference shares	10	9	9
6. Ordinary shares	24	31	51
7. Mortgages	15	18	20
8. Land and buildings	102	104	107
9. Cash	3	3	3
10. Other assets	8	8	7
Total	318	316	334

any figures, and it is impossible to know at all accurately how much property was held by individual churches or regional organizations.

On the basis of this information we estimate that the total property of the Church of England was about £250 m., and that of other denominations about £75 m. An estimate of the distribution between different types of asset is given in Table 53. The accounts of the Church Commissioners are made up on 31 March, those of other bodies at varying dates.

GENERAL CHARITIES

Even the number of these charities in existence is not known

[1] The bodies supplying information were: the Presbyterian Church of England, the Presbyterian Church of Scotland, the British Advent Mission, the Congregational Union, the Congregational Union of Scotland, the Wesleyan Reform Church, the Methodist Church, the United Synagogue, the Board of Deputies of British Jews, and the Baptist Union.

accurately, but there are believed to be about 80,000 of them.[1] Endowed charities, in which the trustees have the use of income only for the purposes of the trust, are supposed to submit copies of their accounts to the Charity Commissioners. Unendowed funds, in which the trustees have the use of both capital and income, are not subject to this obligation. However, even some endowed charities are very lax in their submission of accounts. The Commissioners make no analysis of accounts received and, though the public has the legal right to inspect the accounts of particular charities, the Commissioners refused the general access to the accounts necessary to make a random sample inquiry.

In certain circumstances the assets of charities may be vested in the Official Trustee of Charity Lands or the Official Trustees of Charitable Funds.[2] The holdings of the Official Trustees of Charitable Funds are published in the annual reports of the Charity Commissioners, and the Commissioners kindly supplied me with the following breakdown into various types of security:

Holdings of The Official trustees of Charitable Funds, 31 Dec. 1954

	£'000
British government securities:	
Treasury bills	25
Quoted securities	96,963
Other securities	1,797
Government guaranteed stocks	14,914
Local authorities and public boards	6,051
Canal and water companies	1,557
Dominion, colonial, and foreign stocks	3,159
Debentures and preference shares	1,827
Ordinary shares	1,622
	128,094

There is no valuation available of land and buildings in the hands of the Official Trustee.

The holdings of the Official Trustees, however, cover only a small part of all the assets of charities. The circumstances

[1] *Report of the Committee on the Law and Practice relating to Charitable Trusts* (Nathan Committee), London, H.M.S.O. 1952, Cmd. 8710, para. 103.

[2] For these circumstances, see *Nathan Report*, para. 219 sqq.

in which property is vested in the Official Trustees are such that they get a large number of very small funds but many of the big ones, which make up the greater part of the total, retain the securities in their own hands. The Nathan Committee believed that a majority of charities had their securities vested in the Official Trustees,[1] but this is not borne out by our evidence. The number of accounts held by the Official Trustees is given in Appendix B of the *Annual Report of the Charity Commissioners*. At the end of 1953 it was 73,342. The number of trusts involved was, however, much smaller, as several accounts might be held on behalf of a single trust. We have been assured by the Commissioners that all trusts included in Appendix B would have deposited copies of their accounts with the Commission, and that some trusts deposited accounts even though their securities were not vested in the Official Trustees. The number of separate charities submitting accounts in 1953 was 30,342[2] so the number of separate charities represented in the 73,000 accounts of Appendix B was probably only about 30,000.

The Library of the Family Welfare Association contains a collection of the reports of over 2,000 charities. The Association kindly allowed us to examine these, and we analysed the balance-sheets of all the 324 with assets of over £50,000 and one in eight of these with assets of less than £50,000. The distribution of assets shown by this analysis is given in Table 54.

Where investments were stated to be held by the Official Trustees, they were excluded, but there may be some duplication where investments were so held without it being stated. The list also includes some religious organizations which would be exempt from the jurisdiction of the Commissioners.

The accounts referred to various accounting dates, mostly in 1954. However, a considerable number of accounts were available for several years, and these showed remarkably little variation from year to year either in the amount or the composition of assets. Differences in date are, therefore, likely to be only a minor source of error. Far more serious, however, is the

[1] *Nathan Report*, para. 99.

[2] *Annual Report of the Charity Commissioners*, 1953, p. 4.

fact that the sample is all too evidently biased in favour of the larger institutions.

The last exhaustive survey of charities was by the Brougham Commissions in 1837. They recorded 28,800 charities of which

TABLE 54

The assets of charities and educational foundations as shown by samples of balance-sheets

percentages

	Charities	Educational foundations
1. British Government securities	52·2	35·5
2. Local authorities and public boards	3·9	5·4
3. Overseas securities	1·7	1·0
4. Debentures	2·1	0·6
5. Preference shares	2·4	0·2
6. Ordinary shares	9·2	6·7
7. Mortgages	1·3	1·5
8. Other investments	2·5	0·9
9. Land and buildings	18·0	46·0
10. Cash	4·9	2·2
11. Other assets	1·6	..

23,750 (82·5 per cent.) had an income of less than £30 a year, and 13,330 (46·3 per cent.) an income of less than £5 a year, or a capital of about £100. The Nathan Committee state that 'We believe from such evidence as we have received on this subject that the proportion of small charitable trusts to the present total may be much the same today'.[1] Yet only half a dozen of the balance-sheets we examined had assets of less than £1,000.

Merely to gross up the results of our sample would give a greatly inflated estimate of the total assets of charities, yet there is no direct way by which the bias can be allowed for. It is possible, however, to get a rough idea of the holdings of charities and educational foundations together from the income-tax figures, and this is discussed below.

[1] *Nathan Report*, para. 142.

EDUCATIONAL INSTITUTIONS

The University Grants Committee makes grants to twenty-four university institutions, counting the federal universities of Durham, London, and Wales as single units. Grants are made to the universities of Oxford and Cambridge, but not to the colleges. The annual reports of the Committee give the endowment income of universities, but give no information about their assets.

In reply to our inquiries seventeen universities gave us information though, unfortunately, not all for the same year. From this we prepared a composite statement using figures for the academic years 1952–3 and 1953–4, which is roughly comparable with the University Grants Committee return for 1953–4. Where we were able to get figures for more than one date they showed very little change in investments, so the differences in accounting dates are not likely to be a large source of error.

The universities which gave us information had assets (excluding land and buildings used for teaching) of £16·3 m. and an endowment income in 1953–4 of £408,000. The implied return of only about 2½ per cent. is very low, largely because the universities generally pursue a very conservative investment policy. It is probable, however, that our figures for assets include a certain amount of funds earmarked for special purposes and not included as endowment income by the Grants Committee. In 'grossing-up' the figures we have made some allowance for this by assuming a 3 per cent. yield basis.

The endowment income of all universities in 1953–4 was £1,333,000. The fact that our sample, though covering seventeen out of twenty-four universities, accounts for only about 30 per cent. of income is due to the fact that we could not obtain information from Oxford, Cambridge, or London.

The colleges of Oxford and Cambridge publish a limited amount of information about their income, but nothing about their assets. They derive a high proportion of their income from real property while, so far as their investments are concerned, they vary greatly in policy. A few are known to have ventured boldly into ordinary shares but the majority appear still to adhere to traditional policies of safe investment, with a high proportion of gilt-edged. A study of the accounts of Cambridge colleges for the academic year 1952–3 showed a total income of nearly £964,000, of which £609,000 came from real property and £354,000 from investments. A similar study of the accounts

TABLE 55

The estimated assets of universities

	£m.
1. British government securities	33·9
2. Government guaranteed securities	14·3
3. British local authorities	6·8
4. Overseas securities	3·1
5. Real property	33·2
6. Mortgages	2·1
7. Debenture and preference stocks	2·6
8. Ordinary shares	7·0
9. Other investments	4·6
Total	107·6

of Oxford colleges showed an income of approximately £915,000 from land and buildings, and £475,000 from interest and dividends. We have valued income from real property at twenty-five years' purchase of net rental income (the figure implied in the valuation of the Church Commissioners) and investments on a 3 per cent. yield basis. We have further assumed that college investments are divided between various types of security in the same proportions as those of our sample of universities. The resulting estimates are given in Table 55.

For educational trusts (apart from a very small number of public schools exempted by Act of Parliament) the Ministry of Education has functions similar to those of the Charity Commissioners. The assets of educational trusts, however, if they are not held by the trustees are vested in the Official Trustee of Charity Lands or the Official Trustees of Charitable Funds.

There are about 30,000 educational trusts known to the Ministry, of which about one-third own nothing but a school building. The remainder range from very small funds to rich and famous public schools with assets running into many hundreds of thousands. The difficulties of estimating their assets are similar to those encountered with other charities. The trusts are obliged to deposit accounts with the Ministry, though as with other charities the obligation is not always met. The Ministry does not, however, compile any statistics and did not feel able to let us take a sample of balance-sheets from their files, which they regarded as confidential. They did, however, kindly record for us the names and addresses of all the trusts with which they had correspondence over a period of six weeks. We were thus furnished with a list of 713 names and addresses, to each of which a questionnaire was sent. Two hundred and seventy-five replies were received in a form sufficiently complete for analysis, and it is on the basis of these that the percentages of Table 54 are calculated.

A sample selected by this method is clearly not an ideal one, and it might appear likely that the larger trusts would have more occasion to correspond with the Ministry than would the very small ones. Small funds are much more strongly represented than in our samples of general charities, but they are probably still under-represented, and our guess as to the extent of the under-representation makes a very large difference to our estimate of total assets. Assuming that our sample was entirely representative of the whole population of 20,000 trusts would give them total assets of over £700 m. Assuming that the Brougham Commission's proportions of funds below £600 held good, and that our sample was representative only of funds above that size reduces the estimate to only about £120 m.

The only indication of the total assets both of educational foundations and of charities is that which can be inferred from the income-tax figures. If we assume that all income under Schedules A and D is assessed, and value Schedule A at twenty-five years' purchase of net income and Schedule D on a $5\frac{1}{2}$ per cent. yield basis, we get a total of £475 m. for land and property and £410 m. for assets yielding income assessed under Schedule D. Other exempt bodies account for about £205 m. of property and £225 m. of Schedule D assets, leaving £270 m. of property and £185 m. of Schedule D assets to be divided between charities and educational foundations, other than universities. Our analyses of balance-sheets showed that charities held 18 per cent. of their total resources in property and about 22 per cent. in

TABLE 56

The estimated assets of charities and educational foundations

£ m.

	Charities	*Educational foundations*
1. Government and guaranteed securities	314	124
2. Local authorities and public boards	23	19
3. Overseas securities	10	4
4. Debentures	13	2
5. Preference shares	14	1
6. Ordinary shares	55	23
7. Mortgages	8	5
8. Other investments	15	3
9. Land and buildings	109	161
10. Cash	29	8
11. Other assets	10	..
Total	600	350

Schedule D assets. Educational foundations held 46 per cent. in property and about 15 per cent. in Schedule D assets. If the amount of Schedule A and D assets not otherwise accounted for is divided between the two types of institutions in these proportions charities would hold £110 m. of property and £134 m. of Schedule D assets, while educational foundations would hold £160 m. of property and £52 m. of Schedule D assets. If other assets are related to these in proportions shown by our respective samples, charities would have total resources of around £600 m. and educational foundations of £350 m. In compiling Table 56 we have taken these round figures and distributed them among various types of asset in the proportions shown by our samples.

This method of estimation is clearly only a rough-and-ready one, but it is all that can be done until official statistics are improved. It ignores any income under Schedule D that may escape assessment, and its accuracy depends both on the realism of our valuation of income and on the correctness of our estimates of the resources in property and Schedule D assets of other exempt bodies. The separate estimates for charities and educational foundations would be more affected than would the total of the two by small errors of this kind. For example, if we

TABLE 57. *Friendly societies and collecting societies*

£ *m.*

	1953	*1954*	*1955*
1. British government securities	141	146	152
2. Government guaranteed securities	36	37	39
3. Local authorities and public boards	100	104	108
4. Overseas securities	18	18	19
5. Mortgages	72	75	78
6. Loans on members' policies	1	1	1
7. Land and buildings	45	47	50
8. Cash:			
(*a*) In savings banks	2	2	2
(*b*) Other	3	4	4
9. Other assets	7	8	8
Total	425	441	461

had valued property at twenty years' instead of twenty-five years' purchase of net income, and retained all our other assumptions, the estimate for the two groups combined would have been reduced from £950 m. to £800 m.; but the estimate for educational foundations would have been reduced from £350 m. to £135 m., while that for charities would have been raised from £600 m. to £665 m.

FRIENDLY SOCIETIES

Friendly societies, other than collecting societies, make returns to the Chief Registrar of Friendly Societies. The annual reports of the Chief Registrar give the funds of the societies at the end of each year, and a summary of balance-sheets is provided at five-yearly intervals. The collecting societies make returns to the Industrial Assurance Commissioner, who is the same person as the Chief Registrar, and summaries are published on a similar basis to those of friendly societies. In Table 57 we have adjusted the end-year figures of total funds to give estimates for end-March. In distributing the totals between various types of asset, we have used the quinquennial analyses of balance-sheets together with some additional information given by the Chief Registrar and by the two major societies with branches, the Independent Order of Oddfellows, Manchester Unity, and the Ancient Order of Foresters.

The societies hold about £450 m. of funds, including £150 m. of gilt-edged, nearly £40 m. of nationalization stocks, and about £100 m. of local authority issues. The last figure is rather striking, as it amounts to nearly 20 per cent. of the total amount of local authority issues.

TRADE UNIONS

Trade unions, including employer's associations, are entitled to register as friendly societies. Registration is not compulsory but it is advantageous and apparently very few unions of any size fail to register. Registered unions submit returns to the Chief Registrar of Friendly Societies. The total funds of registered trade unions (including employers associations) were as follows:

£ m. at end-year		
1952	*1953*	*1954*
74·8	71·6	68·4

Part IV of the Chief Registrar's Annual Report for 1953 contains the following percentage breakdown of trade union assets:

	£ *m.*	%
British government securities .	22·4	30·6
British municipal securities .	11·5	15·7
Other investments	24·4	33·2
Mortgages	4·6	6·3
Land and buildings. . . .	2·8	3·8
Cash	6·5	8·9
Other assets	1·1	1·5

The Trade Union Acts allow unions to invest as they like provided that the range of eligible investments is specified in the rules. If the rules do not contain any other provision, however, investment is restricted to trustee securities. The item 'other investments', therefore, probably consists mainly of the stocks of nationalized industries and public boards. In compiling Table 58 we have assumed that this item is made up in the same way as the 'other investments' of the two large collecting societies, of which we were able to get a breakdown.

TABLE 58. *The assets of trade unions*

£ m.

	1953	*1954*	*1955*
1. Government securities	23	22	21
2. Government guaranteed securities	12	12	11
3. Local authorities and public boards	18	17	17
4. Overseas securities	5	5	5
5. Mortgages	5	5	4
6. Land and buildings	3	3	3
7. Cash	7	6	6
8. Other assets	2	2	2
Total	75	72	68

PROFESSIONAL ASSOCIATIONS AND LEARNED SOCIETIES

There are over 400 professional associations and learned societies which are listed in *Whitaker's Almanack*. Questionnaires were sent to a random sample of one in four of these. The proportion of replies was disappointingly low, but thirty-six were received. One, the Royal Society, was so much larger than any of the others that we excluded it from the sample and added it in separately in computing our estimate of the total assets of the group. The remaining thirty-five had total assets as follows:

	£'000	%
Quoted British government securities	1,589	39·6
Savings certificates and defence bonds	42	1·0
Treasury bills	30	0·7
Overseas stocks	103	2·6
Local authorities	151	3·8
Debentures and preference shares	35	0·9
Ordinary shares	141	3·5
Land, buildings, and mortgages	1,300	32·2
Cash	445	11·1
Other assets	181	4·5
	4,016	100

If this sample is representative, the whole group of just over 400 societies would have assets of between £45 m. and £50 m.

LIVERY COMPANIES

There are seventy-nine livery companies listed in *Whitaker*. The 1952 edition gives the income of sixty-four of these, which amounted to £508,000 a year. The twelve 'great companies' accounted for 72·2 per cent. of this. The total assets of the companies would appear to be between £10 m. and £15 m. Questionnaires were sent to these companies on similar lines to those addressed to pension funds and educational charities, but with a much less favourable result. All but a very few of the companies refused information; the few which were kind enough to give it are probably not typical, so it is impossible to form any estimate of the types of property held by the group. However, a large proportion of their funds, which are devoted to charitable and educational purposes, will be covered by our estimates of these organizations. No separate figure has, therefore, been included for their assets.

OTHER CLUBS, SOCIETIES, ETC.

There remains a multitude of clubs and societies furthering the sporting, recreational, or cultural interests of their members. These range all the way from county cricket clubs and the larger football clubs, which may have assets of many thousands of pounds, down to village dramatic societies, mothers' meetings, sewing guilds, and darts clubs with—if they are lucky—a few pounds in the savings bank or in the treasurer's cash box. Their number certainly runs into many hundreds of thousands, and probably into millions. We have looked at a number of them, and found that the larger ones had assets mainly in gilt-edged stock (including defence bonds) while the smaller ones held mainly cash, much of which was in savings banks. It was quite impossible to form any reliable estimate of their assets, and the figure of £50 m. included in our final tables is a purely notional one.

Our estimate of the total assets of charities and non-profit-making organizations is shown in Table 59. It amounts to the formidable sum of more than £2,100 m., including £950 m. of government and government guaranteed securities, £200 m. of local authority stocks, £220 m. of industrial stocks and shares, and £460 m. of real property.

TABLE 59. *The estimated assets of all charities*

	£ m.
	1955
1. British government securities	956
2. Local authorities and public boards	200
3. Overseas securities	49
4. Debenture and preference stocks	46
5. Ordinary shares	138
6. Mortgages	117
7. Loans on members' policies	1
8. Land and buildings	464
9. Cash	83
10. Other assets	50
Total	2,104

11

THE EXTERNAL SECTOR

THE subject of British overseas investments and of overseas investment in Britain offers a wide field for research, which is far beyond the resources available for this study. The present chapter, therefore, merely re-examines already published material to show its relationship to the rest of our results.

Our foreign assets are shown in the matrix tables of Chapter 12 under five headings, foreign governments, British companies operating abroad, foreign companies, currency reserves, and 'other foreign liabilities'. This last item comprises trade credits, acceptances, and liabilities to British policy-holders of overseas life-assurance companies. The main published resources of information are the *Finance Accounts*, for government holdings, and the annual papers *United Kingdom Overseas Investments* published by the Bank of England.

The central government had outstanding advances to allied governments, to Germany and Austria, to colonial governments and to Northern Ireland amounting to £297 m. in 1953, £380 m. in 1954, and £375 m. in 1955 (Chap. 2, Table 2). These figures exclude some £12 m. lent to China which was assumed to have become worthless.

The government also holds shares in the British Petroleum Co. (treated as a British company operating abroad) and in the Suez Canal Company. The Suez Canal shares are given at market value in the *Finance Accounts*, and the B.P. holding (given at cost) has been revalued at market prices. The government also holds in the Exchange Account substantial amounts of the securities of American companies, and the very rough estimate of Chapter 2 (Table 5) has been included among the liabilities of foreign companies. Finally, there are the gold and foreign currency reserves, small foreign debts to government trading agencies, and small holdings of foreign securities in departmental accounts.

The foreign assets of the government may, therefore, be summarized as follows:

£ *m.*

	1953	*1954*	*1955*
Advances to other governments . .	297	380	375
U.K. companies operating abroad .	80	125	210
Foreign companies	207	247	316
Gold and foreign currencies . .	774	959	953
Other foreign liabilities . . .	4	2	1
Total	1,362	1,713	1,855

Some of the public corporations also have substantial interests abroad though, as in the case of companies, it is not always possible to identify them. Cable and Wireless has been treated as a British company operating abroad and its capital entered at the value given in the *Finance Accounts*. Other corporations have investments in overseas subsidiary or associated companies and, where these can be identified from the balance sheets, they have been entered, at book value, as foreign companies. The total amounts are:

£ *m.*

	1953	*1954*	*1955*
Cable and Wireless	30	30	25
Others	13	21	18
Total	43	51	43

For the foreign assets of other British residents, both persons and institutions, we must rely mainly on the Bank of England estimates. These cover investments, 'through the medium of securities quoted on, or otherwise known to, the London Stock Exchange, including U.S. and Canadian dollar market securities on which information is available to the Bank through the operation of Exchange Control'. Holdings of all types of security are in nominal values. The figures are summarized in Table 60.

In order to be consistent with the basis of valuation used in the rest of this study, we revalued the share capital of companies at estimated market value. The Bank of England figures provide a split of share capital by types of company, most of which are closely comparable with similar categories in *Interest and*

Dividends on Securities Quoted on the London Stock Exchange. For British companies operating abroad and for overseas companies other than American we used the ratios of market to nominal values given for each category in *Interest and Dividends*. American shares were valued on a yield basis, using the figures

TABLE 60

Foreign investments of U.K. residents as estimated by the Bank of England

Nominal values £ m. at end-year

	1952	*1953*	*1954*	*1955*
1. Government and municipal loans .	790	799	780	768
2. U.K. companies operating mainly abroad:				
(*a*) Share capital	572	565	652	673
(*b*) Loan capital	78	93	83	80
3. Overseas companies:				
(*a*) Share capital	375	388	429	434
(*b*) Loan capital	167	172	183	182
Total	1,982	2,017	2,127	2,137

of dividends provided by the Bank of England and Mordys' indexes of the yield on stocks. Our market value estimates for 1954 and 1955 are:

	1954	*1955*
	£ m. at end-year	
British companies .	1,763	1,874
Overseas companies .	640	656

Before 1954 our valuation has to be on a much less detailed basis, as explained in Chapter 7.

We can now compare these figures with the estimates which we have made in previous chapters. Since the balance-sheets, from which information about institutional holdings are derived, are scattered through the year, an average of two end-year figures affords the best standard of comparison.

Government and municipal securities

Our previous estimates can be summarized as follows:

£ m.

	1953	1954	1955
Persons . . .	429	385	336
Banks	35	44	53
Insurance companies .	417	415	441
Pension funds . .	54	60	70
Charities . . .	53	51	51
Total . . .	988	955	951

This compares with a Bank of England figure (averaging two years) of £759 m. for 1953, £790 m. for 1954, and £774 m. for 1955. It is clear, therefore, that we have substantially overestimated holdings of this type of asset. There are two possible sources of this error. Our adjustment figure for converting market or balance-sheet values into nominal ones may have been too high. Alternatively, and more probably, our estimate of personal holdings is too high because of distortion introduced by the age factor into the estimates based on estate duty returns. Foreign government and municipal stocks are a type of investment very likely to have been held predominantly by old people, and this could lead to a considerable overestimate.

British companies operating abroad

Our estimates are:

£ m.

	1953	1954	1955
Persons . . .	902	1,106	1,358
Companies . . .	44	47	55
Investment trusts . .	76	101	144
Insurance companies .	180	231	307
Pension funds . .	58	78	99
Charities . . .	16	21	26
Total . . .	1,276	1,584	1,989

The corresponding figure derived from the Bank of England estimates, adjusting share capital for market value, would be about £1,900 m. in 1955. Estimates for 1953 and 1954 are much less reliable, but a reasonable figure would probably be from £1,000 m. to £1,100 m. in 1953 and £1,350–1,450 m. for 1954. Again, our estimate is somewhat too high, and again the discrepancy may be due to error in the estimate of personal holdings. It may also, however, be due to the way in which we have distributed our estimated total holdings of shares between different categories. Neither for persons nor for any of the institutional holders is it possible to distinguish between shares in companies operating mainly abroad and other U.K. companies, so that estimated total holdings have simply been distributed according to the total quantities in existence.

Overseas companies

Our figures are:

£ *m.*

	1953	*1954*	*1955*
Persons . . .	539	618	730
Investment trusts . .	235	316	422
Insurance companies .	70	102	134
Total . . .	844	1,026	1,286

The corresponding figure derived from the Bank of England estimates would be about £1,280 m. for 1955.

There remains the heading of 'other foreign liabilities', in which we have included trade debt, liabilities in respect of life-assurance policies written by foreign companies, and acceptances. Acceptances have been officially valued at the end of the year as follows:

£ *m.*

1952	*1953*	*1954*	*1955*
70	69	102	101[1]

The value of the life-assurance policies has been estimated on the basis of premium income at £120 m. for 1953, £126 m. for 1954, and £135 m. for 1955 (see Chap. 9, p. 112). The figures for

[1] *Economic Trends*, May 1958, p. ix.

trade debt are very tenuous, being simply the residual which remains after distributing the 'trade debtors' items in the balance-sheets of companies and public corporations as explained in the notes to Chapter 12. The results of this process are:

£ *m.*		
1953	*1954*	*1955*
403	436	486

Finally, there are about £11 m. of 'overseas balances' shown in the balance-sheets of the banks, which we have included with currency reserves.

Estimated foreign assets for 1955 are summarized in Table 61. It must be remembered that these figures are based on the nominal values of fixed charge loans and the estimated market values of ordinary shares. They probably represent a minimum figure even for the assets shown, as there are almost certainly some investments which escape the observation of the Bank. Moreover, they omit one very important class of asset, the foreign assets of companies classed as operating mainly in the United Kingdom.

Unfortunately there is no way of estimating the overseas assets of U.K. companies. If they were provided in a somewhat different form, the estimates of income might provide a valuable clue, but as it is they are useless. The total interest and dividends received on investments known to the Bank of England in 1955 was £207 m. The total 'interest, profits and dividends' recorded in the Balance of Payments White Paper was £337 m. However, the Bank of England figure includes some foreign taxation excluded in the White Paper, but takes no account of undistributed profits, included in the White Paper. In order to get a figure comparable with that of the White Paper, it would be necessary to add to the Bank of England figure the undistributed profits of U.K. companies operating abroad and to subtract overseas tax payments. If this could be done the difference between the two figures would give a useful indication of the magnitude of assets not covered by the Bank of England survey. Since neither of these items is known, however, nothing can be done.

The omission of the overseas assets of companies operating in Britain from this section does not, however, lead to an under-estimate of the total assets of companies. These assets are included in the balance-sheets which form the basis of Chapter 7,

TABLE 61

Estimated foreign assets

£ m.

	1955	
1. Overseas governments and municipalities:		
(*a*) Held by government . . .	375	
(*b*) Held by other British residents	774	
		1,149
2. British companies operating mainly abroad:		
(*a*) Government and public corporations .	235	
(*b*) Others	1,900	
		2,135
3. Overseas companies:		
(*a*) Government and public corporations . . .	333	
(*b*) Others	1,330	
		1,663
4. Currency reserves:		
(*a*) Government	935	
(*b*) Others	11	
		946
5. Other foreign liabilites:		
(*a*) Government	1	
(*b*) Acceptances	101	
(*c*) Insurance policies	135	
(*d*) Trade debtors	486	
		723
		6,616

so that we have included as domestic assets some which should have been classed as overseas.

British foreign liabilities are, if possible, even more shrouded in mystery than are our assets. Only one item, the loans raised abroad by the government, is perfectly clear and straightforward. The *Finance Accounts* classify the debt according to whether it is payable in external currencies or in sterling. We discussed this in Chapter 2 and in Table 7 reclassified the debt so as to show separately debt payable in sterling but to overseas lenders. The summary figures were:

£ m.	1953	1954	1955
External sterling debt:			
International institutions . .	758	693	510
Other	99	96	96
Debt payable in foreign currencies:			
International institutions . .	..	..	59
Other	2,163	2,115	2,071
Total	3,020	2,904	2,736

The heading 'international institutions' comprises the International Monetary Fund, the International Bank for Reconstruction and Development (World Bank), and the European Payments Union. Obligations to these institutions are of two distinct kinds, though they are not separated in the figures. The Treasury notes deposited with these institutions in payment (or part payment) of our initial subscription are liabilities from a balance of payments point of view, in that the institutions (in circumstances provided for in their rules) can cash them and lend the proceeds for spending by foreigners. On the other hand, this process would give rise to a right to repayment (in circumstances provided for by the rules) and so would create a net asset. We cannot, therefore, regard these notes as part of the net indebtedness of the country, any more than we could regard an uncalled liability on a share as part of the net indebtedness of the shareholder. Notes created by drawings on international institutions are, however, quite different; they are a form of borrowing which creates a specific obligation to repay, and they ought to be regarded as part of net indebtedness. From the point of view of our debts to the rest of the world, therefore, our initial subscription to I.M.F. and the World Bank, amounting to £452 m., ought to be deducted from the above figures.

The other external debt includes small amounts of colonial savings certificates and other securities likely to be held by persons, but is almost all loans from foreign governments. By far the largest items are, of course, the U.S. loan under the financial agreement of December 1945, and the similar Canadian loan of March 1946. These stood, respectively, at £1,478 m. and £411 m. in 1955.

Besides these loans actually raised abroad, there are, of course, large amounts both of Treasury bills and of quoted government securities held overseas, mostly in the so-called sterling balances. These balances are officially defined as including the following four categories:

(i) Holdings in sterling or sterling area currencies (whether as deposits, advances or commercial bills or Treasury bills, or British government securities if held for account of overseas banks) of account holders abroad with banks in the United Kingdom; net of claims of similar types by banks in the United Kingdom on overseas banks and other residents abroad (i.e. the sum of the three sub-totals referred to above).

(ii) Funds, now small, held for account of the United States government, for their own use or for help to third countries, originating from the sterling equivalent of dollars made available under United States aid legislation.

(iii) Sterling funds held with the Crown Agents for Oversea Governments and Administrations and by currency boards, excluding Dominion and Colonial sterling securities.

(iv) So far as known, British government securities held by other official bodies but not those held by private individuals or firms.

Until recently, nothing was known about the composition of these balances. In May 1958, however, there was published an analysis of holdings of 'central banks and other official agencies' (comprising over three-quarters of the total) at the end of 1956.[1] This gave the following percentage figures:

	%
Bank deposits	8
Treasury bills	32
Government securities maturing in	
Under 5 years	28
5–10 years	9
10–15 years	14
Over 15 years	9
	100

[1] *Economic Trends*, May, 1958, p. ix.

This, however, is an imperfect guide to previous years, both because non-official holdings may be very different in composition from official ones, and because holdings change considerably over time. This can happen through individual holders switching from one asset to another in response to changing market conditions. It can also happen through changes in the relative importance of different holders; even though the total amount might change little some holders may run down their balances and others (possibly with different asset preferences) increase them.

The amount of the balances, excluding those of the non-territorial organizations, was £3,609 m. in June 1953, £3,823 in 1954, and £3,691 m. in 1955. Thus, if the proportions given for official holdings at the end of 1956 could, in spite of what has been said above, be assumed to hold good for all balances in 1955, they would have comprised about £295 m. of cash, £1,180 m. of Treasury bills, and £2,215 m. of quoted government securities.

There is indirect evidence, however, that non-official holders had a smaller proportion of government securities than official ones.

Overseas balances are known to figure largely in the short-term borrowing of the discount market. The total amount of this short-term borrowing varies greatly from time to time, with fluctuations in the Treasury bill issue. In March 1955 there was a gap of £550 m. between the total borrowings of the market and our estimate of their borrowing from British banks. Since the discount houses rank as reporting banks for this purpose most, if not all, of their foreign borrowing should appear in the sterling balances, and most of this would probably be drawn from non-official funds. The breakdown between official and non-official funds is available only for the end of 1945 (£807 m.), 1951 (£660 m.), and 1957 (£759 m.). These funds could, therefore, have supplied most for the borrowing by the discount market for which we have not accounted otherwise, but this would have implied that a high proportion of them was employed in this way. In fact it is known that other domestic institutions (including local authorities and some large firms) do appear both as borrowers and lenders in the short loan market, and our unallocated figure probably includes some domestic lending. Even so, it seems likely that non-official funds hold only a low proportion of gilt-edged, and that the total amount in the sterling balances was less than the £2,215 m. mentioned above.

The unallotted residual in our estimates consists of £1,765 m. of Treasury bills and £1,488 m. of quoted government stocks. There was, however, also a residual of £444 m. of the securities of public corporations, though our estimate of internal holdings of local authority stocks comes to £72 m. more than the total in existence. Both of these are held to some extent by currency boards and other holders of sterling balances, though the amounts are limited by the fact that these stocks have fairly distant redemption dates. Thus, our total residual for public sector securities is reasonably consistent with what is known about the sterling balances, on the assumption that foreign holdings outside the balances were small. It appears, however, that we have probably underestimated domestic holdings of Treasury bills and correspondingly overestimated holdings of quoted gilt-edged.

The sterling balances include bank deposits and securities held by foreigners through reporting banks net of similar claims by the banks on foreign account. Gross liabilities of the banks to foreigners would exceed this figure by the amount of foreign assets held by the banks on their own behalf or on behalf of customers.

Liabilities of British life-assurance companies to foreign policy holders have been estimated at £213 m. in 1953, £246 m. in 1954, and £275 m. in 1955 on the basis of premium income. Foreign insurance companies doing business in Britain are shown in their returns to the Board of Trade as holding the following amounts of British government and guaranteed securities:

£ *m.*

1953	*1954*	*1955*
98	102	99

There remains foreign holdings of real assets in Britain and holdings of stocks and shares in British registered companies.

No information is available on direct foreign holdings of real assets, but this is probably not large. Some foreign individuals obviously own property in Britain and some foreign firms have branches or offices here which are not registered as companies; almost all the large units are, however, registered either as public or private companies.

Our estimates of the assets and liabilities of companies, especially of private companies, are subject to so large an error that the residual item is of no real help here, and the direct evidence on foreign holdings is very scanty. A study of the hundred largest companies listed by the National Institute of Economic and Social Research showed known holdings by overseas companies with a market value, at mid 1954, of about £165 m. Mr. J. H. Dunning, in his study, *American Investment in British Manufacturing Industry*, found total U.S. investments of $1,420 m. (£550 m.) in 1955.[1] It is not quite clear how this value was calculated, but it appears to be on a basis of balance-sheet value of net assets. It included only the holdings of parent companies in British companies where the American share was more than 25 per cent. It takes no account, of course, of investment by non-American overseas companies of holdings by American Companies amounting to less than 25 per cent., or of private holdings of the shares of British companies, all of which must have been substantial.

A further clue can be gained from the figures of property income paid abroad, though again the position is complicated by taxation. The balance-of-payments White Paper shows 'interest profits and dividends' paid abroad in 1955 net of U.K. tax of £274 m. Most of the overseas loans of the government are at a low rate of interest, and the total interest payment shown in the Finance Accounts for 1955 is only £50 m. On the basis of the composition of sterling balances discussed earlier and the prevailing deposit, discount, and gilt-edged rates, the gross interest on sterling balances in 1955 may be estimated at about £120 m. A good deal of this, though not all, would be

[1] J. H. Dunning, *American Investment in British Manufacturing Industry*, London: Allen & Unwin, 1958, p. 52.

net of tax to non-residents. Thus earning assets outside the sterling balances must have produced over £100 m. net of tax. These assets would include interest on government securities held outside the sterling balances, dividends on shares in British companies, remitted profits of overseas companies, and 'a small amount of profits retained for re-investment'. It appears likely that investments in British companies form the largest part. Companies studied by the Board of Trade in 1955 paid dividends (net of tax) amounting to an average of under 3·4 per cent. on the balance-sheet value of shareholders' interests in net assets; on a market value basis the yield would have been rather lower. It is thus difficult to put foreign assets outside the sterling balances at much less than £3,000 m.

We may sum up our very tentative conclusions as follows: government borrowing abroad, excluding our quota subscriptions to the I.M.F. and the World Bank, was £2,284 m. in 1955. The sterling balances accounted for a further £3,700 m. Other earning assets held by foreigners can be very tentatively put at around £3,000 m. on the basis of income earned; a few hundred million of this would be in public sector securities, but most of it was probably in British companies, public and private. Finally, there was a liability of British life-assurance companies to foreign policy holders of about £275 m. Total foreign liabilities must have amounted to over £9,000 m. against the £6,600 m. of assets shown in Table 61. It must be remembered, however, that Table 61 understates the credit position by omitting the foreign assets of British companies operating mainly at home.

12

THE STRUCTURE OF OWNERSHIP

WE now bring together the information described in Chapters 2 to 11 in the form of combined accounts for the economy as a whole. These are shown in Tables 62 to 65. The tables give combined, rather than consolidated, accounts as in general a sectors' holding of its own liabilities is shown in the appropriate place. Each vertical column gives the assets of a particular sector according to the sector of which they are a liability. The totals at the foot of the tables thus show the gross assets of each sector and, if the sector's holdings of its own liabilities are deducted, we have its holdings of real assets and claims on the rest of the economy. Where an item is entered at a different value from that of the balance-sheet or other source from which our earlier estimates have been compiled, this is allowed for in the 'adjustment' item at the foot of the table, so that the adjusted vertical totals correspond with the totals of appropriate tables in Chapters 2 to 11. These adjustments are given in detail in the notes to the tables. Each horizontal line shows the way in which the liabilities of a sector (in some cases a particular type of liability) are distributed among different holders, and the totals on the right-hand side of the tables correspond to the total liabilities shown in the appropraite tables of Chapters 2 to 11.

In the previous tables we have used the basis of valuation adopted in our source material; book values in most cases, market values in a few including persons, investment trusts, and pension funds. Our choice of categories has also been largely determined by our source material in that, where assets in two or more of our present categories have been combined in our source material, we have not attempted to split them. It is now necessary to make adjustments, as best we can, to meet both these difficulties.

For reasons explained in Chapter 1, it is not possible to adopt a single logically consistent basis of valuation for all assets, though it is obviously desirable that any particular type of asset should be valued on the same basis throughout. The following principles have been adopted here:

(*a*) All fixed interest stocks and shares, mortgages and other loans, trade debt, hire-purchase balances, and bank deposits have been taken at their nominal value.

(*b*) All ordinary stocks and shares have been taken at estimated market value.

(*c*) For fixed assets it has, unfortunately, not been possible to be consistent throughout. Where balance-sheet data have been available—for parts of the central government sector, for public corporations, local authorities, and companies—book values have been used. For personal property, the basis has of necessity to be market value as estimated for death duties, while for charities and in a few other minor cases it has been necessary to use a notional figure inferred from income.

Where the valuation used in our source material differs from this, adjustments have been made, the methods and amounts of which are given in the notes to the tables. Where assets in several of our present categories are combined in the source material, an estimated distribution has been made. Where possible, we have drawn on known investment policy, e.g. the banks often-stated preference for short-dated investments, or upon evidence from similar types of institution. Where no such evidence is available, it has been assumed that assets are distributed between categories in proportion to the total amount of each outstanding. Again, details of the methods used are given in the notes.

The totals in the right-hand column are normally the balance-sheet liabilities of the sector concerned. Where balance-sheets, either actual or estimated, have not been available we have tried to show an estimate of the total liability which is independent of the identified items shown in previous columns. This has been done for foreign governments and companies and for stocks. For persons, charities, fixed assets, and 'other foreign liabilities', however, no suitable independent figure is available, and the totals for these are merely the sum of our identified items.

If our estimates were perfect the cross totals of each line would, of course, equal the corresponding figure in the right-hand column, and imperfections in the estimates will show up in the 'unalloted' column. Unfortunately, these imperfections are of several kinds. First, there are balance-sheet items, e.g. 'provisions', which it was impossible to allocate as assets to any other sector; these are listed fully in the notes. Secondly, we have no satisfactory estimate of foreign holdings of British assets, other than loans from foreign governments and liabilities to international financial institutions. All other foreign holdings, including those in the sterling balances, are thus comprised in unallocated items. Finally, of course, there are ordinary errors and omissions. In spite of this difficulty, however, the presentation of the figures in this form does give some check on the adequacy of our estimates.

It we consider the floating debt, and the quoted securities of the central government, public corporations, and local authorities together, our unallocated items are (as explained in Chapter 11) consistent with what is known about foreign holdings, particularly those in the sterling balances. It appears, however, that we have rather overestimated domestic holdings of quoted securities and underestimated Treasury bills. This is probably due to the inadequacy of our information about the short-term assets of companies and of banks other than the clearing and Scottish banks, and to the fact that we have made no allowance for 'tender' Treasury bills that may be held by the Bank of England and other official funds. There is a fairly large unallocated amount of 'other internal debt'. A large part of this is the 5 per cent. of small savings securities assumed to be outside personal hands, most of which could not be traced. There is also a small discrepancy between 'other capital liabilities' and the amount shown under this heading in published departmental accounts, which is, presumably, held in unpublished accounts. The 'other liabilities' of public corporations and local authorities represent balance-sheet items, listed in the notes, that cannot be treated as the assets of any other sector.

The treatment of the shares of public companies is much complicated by problems of valuation, especially in the case of ordinary shares. When they appear as assets, these shares have been entered at estimated market value. The 'Unallocated' column shows the difference between our estimate of the holdings of all domestic sectors and the estimated market value of quoted ordinary shares (Chapter 7, Table 34) plus an allowance for unquoted public companies. The 'adjustment' item represents the difference between this figure and the estimated balance-sheet value of ordinary capital and reserves (Chapter 7, Table 36). The balance-sheet value of capital and reserves depends, of course, largely on the book value of real assets. Fixed assets are normally valued on the basis of cost on acquisition less depreciation, with only rare revaluations. After nearly twenty years of rising prices, therefore, book values would be well below replacement cost. Yet even in the 1955 boom, the market value of ordinary shares was slightly less than the book value of ordinary capital and reserves; for earlier years, under the combined influence of stock-market pessimism and dividend restraint, there was a very wide gap. It could be argued that market values were distorted by the reluctance of directors to pay out a reasonable proportion of earnings in ordinary dividends, a reluctance that was fortified by official exhortation and by discriminatory taxes. The alternative would be to accept the market valuation as a fair assessment of prospective earnings, which would lead to the conclusion that a large part of the capital of British industry was incapable of earning an economic return on its replacement cost.

Coming back to our figures, the unallocated items in the capital of non-financial public companies are as follows:

£ *m.*

	1953	*1954*	*1955*
Debentures . .	142	242	264
Preference shares .	−107	−45	93
Ordinary shares .	−160	206	1,019

The amount unallocated rises very sharply in 1955, implying that the increase in our basis of valuation did not fully keep up with the rise in the price of ordinary shares. Since the mid-1955 valuation came almost at the peak of the Stock Exchange boom, this is not surprising. Even in 1955, however, the residual is not overlarge in relation to the probable size of foreign holdings, discussed in Chapter 11. The market valuations are subject to a certain amount of error, particularly that for 1953, but even so it seems virtually certain that we have overestimated the value of domestic holdings of ordinary shares in 1953 and 1954. The most probable source of such an error is again in the estimate of personal holdings.

The unallocated liabilities of private companies appear very large. They include the 'other liabilities' of Chapter 7, Table 37, but unallocated capital and reserves amounted to £1,751 m. in 1953, £2,114 m. in 1954, and no less than £2,588 m. in 1955. The big jump from 1954 to 1955 is due to the combination of an increase in estimated capital and a decline in estimated personal holdings. The presence of a large unallocated item is not surprising, as much of the foreign industrial investment discussed in Chapter 11 would be in subsidiaries of foreign firms registered as private companies. Even so, however, the figures we have reached are too large to be plausible, and it seems likely that the very crude methods described in Chapter 7 have led us to overestimate both the size and the rate of growth of the balance-sheet totals for private companies. It is impossible, however, to reach any certainty on this point until a study can be made of a representative sample of private company balance-sheets.

There is little which calls for special comment in the liabilities of non-banking financial institutions. Again, adjustment items occur in appropriate places to denote the difference between the estimated market value of shares and the balance-sheet value of capital and reserves. The unallocated capital and reserves of banks, insurance companies, and investment trusts follow a similar pattern to those of non-financial public companies; the unallocated sum for 1955 seems to represent a reasonable allowance for foreign holdings, but the estimates of domestic holdings for 1953 and 1954 seem rather high. The large unallocated item for insurance companies includes the estimated liabilities of life offices on foreign policies, and the whole of non-life insurance funds. The remaining unallocated items are described in the notes.

Our estimate of fixed assets is on the basis of valuation for probate (based on market value) for persons; balance-sheet values for the government, public corporations, and companies; net loan debt for local authorities and capitalization of income for charities. This hotch-potch of different methods of valuation is obviously unsatisfactory, but was dictated by the nature of the source material. The total in the right-hand column of the table is simply the sum of the preceding items.

Despite differences both in coverage and valuation, it is interesting to compare our figures with the two other post-war estimates made by Mr. Redfern and Dr. Barna.[1] Both these aim to calculate the replacement value of assets, though by very different methods.

Redfern uses a 'perpetual inventory' method, which involves estimating gross investment each year for a period covering the whole life of the asset in question, deducting accrued depreciation, and correcting for price changes. Dr. Barna uses information supplied to him directly by firms and based mainly on the value for which they insured their assets against fire. Redfern's coverage is largely, though not entirely, the same as ours; Barna's is much narrower, including only manufacturing industry.

The main differences in coverage between Redfern's figures and ours are that he omits consumers' durable goods and furniture, goodwill, land and site values, farm buildings, coal industry buildings and mine workings, and central government non-trading assets (apart from those concerned with the armed

[1] P. Redfern, 'Net Investment in Fixed Assets in the United Kingdom, 1938–53', *J.R.S.S.*, series A, part ii, 1955, pp. 141–82, and T. Barna, 'The Replacement Cost of Fixed Assets in British Manufacturing Industry in 1955', ibid., series A, part i, 1957, pp. 1–36.

forces, which are omitted by both of us). We omit assets owned directly by foreigners which would, presumably, be included by his method. Redfern's estimate of the net value of capital at replacement cost at the end of 1953 is £24,427 m. at 1948 prices, which would be equivalent to just over £31,000 m. in 1953. Our own estimates, by the methods of valuation already described, was £21,836 m. in 1953 and £23,020 m. in 1954. Redfern found that, for public utilities and manufacturing industry, net values on 1952 replacement cost were 1·6 to 1·7 times those on an original cost basis. Our own estimate of the value of local authority housing by Mr. Redfern's method gave a value 40 per cent. above that on a net loan debt basis (which roughly corresponds to original cost less depreciation). For older houses, the difference would be even greater. It would seem, therefore, that we should add at least 65 per cent. to the assets we have valued on an original cost less depreciation basis to bring them to 1953 replacement cost. These assets were around £15,000 m. at our valuations so that revaluing on a replacement cost basis would add around £10,000 m. to our total, bringing it to between £32,000 m. and £33,000 m. for the end of 1953. Even this is by no means a generous margin for the differences in coverage, but the figures are probably as close as one could expect when such diverse sources and such large margins of error are involved.

Dr. Barna, however, has produced a much higher estimate of capital in manufacturing industry. After adjusting for differences in coverage, he found that his own estimates were about 57 per cent. higher than those of Mr. Redfern, a discrepancy which he attributes mainly to the difficulty of compiling statistics of investment and of prices over the long period of history required for the Redfern method. Our own research has not been of a kind which would enable us to criticize Barna's method or to assess its reliability as compared with that of Redfern. All we can say is that while our figures can be made to square with those of Redfern on quite plausible assumptions, we should have to suppose a very high ratio of replacement cost to book value in order to reconcile them with those of Barna.

For stocks our figures are rather higher than those of the

National Income Blue Book, and this point has been discussed in Chapter 7.

In the case of overseas assets, the totals in the right-hand column are derived from the Bank of England estimates of overseas investments. These have been adjusted by valuing share capital at estimated market value; by adding foreign loans made by the central government to the Bank of England figures of government and municipal loans; and by adding securities held in the Exchange Account and by the public corporations, overseas companies, and British companies operating abroad, as appropriate. The reconciliation of these figures with our other estimates was discussed in Chapter 11, where it appeared that our estimate for foreign companies checked up very well, but that those for government and municipal loans and for British companies operating abroad were probably on the high side.

For the categories discussed so far, our estimates seem to be reasonably consistent with one another and with such independent information as we have. Where it does appear that we have erred in our estimates of domestic assets, that error generally seems to be in the upward direction. This makes the very large underestimate of holdings of cash all the more surprising.

The total amounts of cash which we estimate to exist outside the banking system at the end of March each year was:

	1953	*1954*	*1955*
Notes and coin	1,364	1,417	1,552
Bank of England 'other' deposits	75	73	66
Clearing and Scottish banks .	6,300	6,503	6,577
Other banks . . .	695	730	789
Total	8,434	8,723	8,984
Allocated to domestic sector .	4,157	4,272	4,209
	4,277	4,451	4,775

The figure for clearing-bank deposits differs from the totals of Tables 62–64 by the amount of the seasonal adjustment.

These figures have been adjusted so as to avoid duplication so far as possible. Bank deposits are net of 'collections' and balances with other banks, and also of estimated items in transit between branches (see Chap. 8). Deposits with, and loans to, the discount houses are not included.

The allocation of the 'cash' item in a balance-sheet between different types of cash is bound to be arbitrary, so it is best to consider the total figure.

Overseas holdings can account for only a small proportion of our unallocated item. At the end of 1956 only 8 per cent. of the official sterling balances was held in the form of bank deposits. This would amount to less than £250 m. and some of this may have been in loans to the discount market rather than deposits in our present sense. Unofficial balances were running at about £700 m. and, as explained in Chapter 11, it seems likely that a considerable part of these were loans to the discount market. Thus total foreign holdings of bank deposits in the sterling balances can hardly have exceeded £500 m. The figures of sterling balances are based on banks' reporting of their net foreign liabilities, so that we should add the amount of their claims, on behalf of themselves and their customers on overseas firms. No information is available about this figure, but it would be surprising if it were large in relation to the magnitudes for which we have to account.

We are thus left with between £3,500 m. and £4,000 m. of cash—nearly half the total amount outstanding—unaccounted for. It is possible to suggest various ways in which part of this discrepancy could arise but it is very difficult to account convincingly for the whole of it.

The estimate of the total amount of cash outstanding is firmly based on balance-sheet data except for the merchant banks. Here, an estimate was obtained by multiplying the balance-sheet figures of five banks by a rather arbitrary figure of four (see Chap. 8). This multiplier may have been too high but, since our estimated deposits with merchant banks reached a maximum of £330 m., the error must have been comparatively small. The main trouble is clearly an underestimate of holdings, rather than an overestimate of the amount of cash in existence.

The estate-duty returns proved valueless as a means of estimating personal holdings of notes and coin, and our figure was based on what seemed a reasonable proportion of income to keep in currency for ordinary transactions (see Chap. 6). It does not allow for personal hoards, but it would be necessary to assume a very great amount of hoarding in order to account for any large part of our gap. It is, of course, impossible to make any allowance for notes lost or held abroad, and one cannot even guess at how large this figure may be.

While our figure of bank deposits is net of items in transit, it includes some internal accounts (e.g. those of staff pension funds) which it is impossible to separate. These are generally believed to be small; they may be larger than we think but it is hard to believe that they could fill much of the gap.

The estimate of personal holdings of bank deposits is based, as explained in Chapter 6, on the returns of net personal deposits by the clearing banks, and the adjustments for other banks and for conversion from net to gross deposits should not involve large errors. The omission of non-corporate business deposits may, however, account for a quite substantial sum.

Our figures for private companies are very tentative and we have already seen that there are strong reasons for supposing that we have underestimated their debt to the banks. It is possible that we may have underestimated their creditor position too; there is such diversity among them that some may have had large cash balances (by the standards of public companies) while others had large overdrafts, but this does not seem a very plausible hypothesis.

The figures for public companies are derived, with only minor modifications, from balance-sheets, so that the error here cannot be large unless the balance-sheets fail to represent the true position. It has been suggested to me that this might be so in that some companies may 'window-dress' not for liquidity but for illiquidity. A large cash item in the balance-sheet could be taken as evidence that the resources of the firm were not being fully used, and so as a reflection on the energy and initiative of the board; it might tempt shareholders to ask for higher dividends, and it might, of course, stimulate a take-over bid. It is possible that some directors, wishing to avoid any of these risks, might arrange the affairs of their firm so that its cash was at a low ebb at the end of its financial year, but again it is difficult to imagine this happening on a very large scale.

There are, however, two other reasons why balance-sheets may not tell the full story of the cash position. Where a firm has several bank accounts (as is very common), or where the accounts of a subsidiary company are consolidated with the parent, the cash item is, of course, net. Hence, if some accounts are overdrawn while others are in credit, the total both of cash and overdrafts would appear smaller in the balance-sheets than in the figures of the banks. Secondly, it appears to be customary to deduct the value of cheques paid from the company's cash balance when the cheques are drawn and to add the value of cheques received only when they are actually paid into the bank. In this way quite substantial sums representing cheques in the post and cheques received but not yet paid in may have been omitted.

Finally, there is the possibility that we may have underestimated the cash held by charities, though there is nothing in the many accounts which we examined to suggest that this is so.

The question of who holds cash is a crucial one for the study of the banking system and for the analysis of how monetary policy works, yet our study has been able only to emphasize the mystery. Probably little more can be done until the Bank of England and the commercial banks produce more detailed figures, and it is to be hoped that this will not be long delayed.

NOTES TO TABLES 62–65

CENTRAL GOVERNMENT (Chapter 2)

Floating debt. (Chapter 2, Table 6, item 1*d*.)

Quoted securities. Chapter 2, Table 3, item 1*b*, and estimated Bank of England holding from Table 6, item 2*d*.

Other national debt. The difference between the two previous items and the total of Table 6. This equals the unquoted securities in published accounts (Table 3, item 1*c*), plus the discrepancy between Table 3 and the *National Debt Return*, including that due to annuities.

Bank of England. Public deposits plus capital valued as in the Exchequer Accounts (Table 2, item 1*b*).

Public corporations. Securities are departmental holdings (Table 3, item 2) plus the nominal capital of Cable and Wireless (Table 2, item 2*f*). Loans are entered as they stand in the accounts of the corporations (Chapter 3, Table 15, item 1*c*). Owing to differences in timing this amount is smaller than the corresponding item in the exchequer return. The difference, included in the adjustment item, is:

	£ *m.*	
1953	*1954*	*1955*
30	14	49

Other liabilities are taxation and interest and dividends (Chapter 3, Table 15, items 1*e* and *d*). Since interest and dividends are not included in the government accounts, they have also been entered, as a negative item, in the adjustment.

Local authorities. Securities as in Chapter 2, Table 5, item 4*b*. Loans as in Chapter 4, Table 25, item 1. The difference between this and the figure at which loans stand in the Exchequer Accounts, included in the adjustment item, is:

	£ *m.*	
1953	*1954*	*1955*
48	41	37

Persons. Persons are assumed to be responsible for a quarter of outstanding income-tax, as shown in the Inland Revenue Reports, and the whole of outstanding surtax and 'special contribution'.

Companies operating in the U.K. Securities of British Sugar Corporation (Chapter 2, Table 2, item 4*a*). 'Other liabilities' of companies are debts to trading agencies and taxation. The whole of the non-government trade debtors' item in the balance-sheets of trading agencies (Chapter 2, Table 1, item 5*c*) are assumed to be due from companies. Companies' tax liabilities are taken from our combined balance sheets (Chapter 7, Table 36, item 7*d*, and Table 37, item 5).

The External Sector. Loans to foreign governments, from Chapter 2, Table 2, items *5c–f*. The British Petroleum Company Ltd. is treated as a British company operating abroad; the government's holding of ordinary shares is entered at estimated market value, which is, of course, far greater than the value (at cost) in the Finance Accounts (Chapter 2, Table 2, item *5a*). The resulting adjustment is:

	£ *m.*	
1953	*1954*	*1955*
−75	−120	−205

The Suez Canal Company is treated as a foreign company. Curiously enough its shares are shown at market value in the Finance Accounts, so no adjustment is necessary. The estimated holding of dollar securities by the Exchange Account are shown as liabilities of foreign companies.

Real assets are as in Chapter 2, Table 8, item 8.

Unidentified items. The 'securities' item in the balance-sheet of the Bank of England is included here. These securities consist of Treasury bills, trade bills, and other securities in unknown proportions.

Total. The total assets of the central government, including the adjustment item, are equal to the total shown in Chapter 2, Table 8, plus internal holdings of the national debt (Table 6) plus the capital and public deposits of the Bank of England.

PUBLIC CORPORATIONS (Chapter 3)

Figures derived from Table 15.

Government securities were adjusted to estimated nominal value, and the resulting addition entered (with a minus sign) in the adjustment item:

	£ *m.*	
1953	*1954*	*1955*
10	5	14

Trade debt. Debt outstanding to the gas and electricity authorities on hire-purchase agreements is treated as a liability of the personal sector. Other trade debt is assumed to be due from companies.

Securities and trade investments were distributed between the debentures, preference shares, and ordinary shares of companies as indicated by the investment schedules of the corporations concerned, largely the Iron & Steel Holding & Realisation Agency.

Unidentified items. Deficiencies and 'other assets' (item 11).

LOCAL AUTHORITIES (Chapter 4)

Government securities are adjusted for nominal value. The amount added was:

	£ *m.*	
1953	*1954*	*1955*
18	12	17

Liabilities in respect of hospitals are allocated to the central government, and those in respect of other transferred services to the public corporations. The difference between the figure at which these appear in Local Government Financial Statistics and in the accounts of the corporations is incorporated in the adjustment item. It was £6 m. in 1953 and 1954 and £4 m. in 1955.

Total assets, allowing for these adjustments, correspond to the total of Chapter 4, Table 25, plus the internal loans and holdings of local authority securities shown in Table 18, items 12 and 15.

PERSONS (Chapter 6)

Central government. Quoted government securities are entered at estimated market value in Table 30, so that no further adjustment is needed. 'Other internal debt' consists of small savings securities (of which 95 per cent. are assumed to be held by persons) and post-war credits.

Public corporations. 'Other liabilities' consist of deposits in railway savings banks and deposits with the corporations by their pension funds; these are included respectively in items 11*b* and 9 of Table 30.

Local authorities. 'Other liabilities' are pension rights under local authority schemes (part of Table 30, item 9). As these schemes, unlike those of the public corporations, are included in the accounts of the authorities, the whole assets of the funds appear here.

Persons. The whole of 'Mortgages and other debts' (Table 30, item 6) is treated as person to person liabilities.

Companies. Shares in public companies (Table 30, item 4*a*) have been divided between debentures, preference shares, and ordinary shares of non-financial companies, and capital of various types of financial company in proportion to the total market value in each category.

Shares, loans and deposits, and 'sundry funds' of the co-operative societies (Chapter 7, Table 38, items 1, 2, and 4) are treated as assets of the personal sector. These form part of item 10 of Table 30.

Banks. Commercial bank deposits, item 11*a*, are distributed between clearing banks and other banks in proportion to the total deposits of each.

Insurance companies. Item 8 is the value of life-assurance policies taken from the returns of the companies. It comprises the liabilities to policy-holders of British companies less an allowance for the foreign business, plus the estimated liabilities to British policy-holders of overseas companies. The latter is included among the 'other liabilities' of the external sector.

The remaining liabilities of financial institutions (apart from deposits with building societies) that are estimated holdings of the capital by persons, allocated as described above.

Adjustments. The entry in this column represents the difference between item 10 of Table 30 and the total of shares and deposits of building societies (Chapter 9, Table 48, items 1 and 2) and personal assets in co-operative societies.

NON-FINANCIAL COMPANIES (Chapter 7).

Public companies (Table 36).

Central government. Investments (item 14) have been distributed between Treasury bills, quoted government securities and 'other investments' according to the proportions shown in balance-sheets analysed by the National Institute of Economic and Social Research. 'Other investments' are placed in the 'unidentified items' line.

Other internal debt is companies' holding of Tax Reserve Certificates (item 15) less a seasonal adjustment which appears in the adjustment line.

Government trading agencies. This is the estimated liabilities to companies of government trading agencies, and forms part of item 13. The total 'trade creditors' of government agencies is distributed between public and private companies in proportion to their 'trade debtors'.

Public corporations. 'Other liabilities' are quoted companies' share of the 'trade creditors' of public corporations (Chapter 3, Table 13, item 2*b*) distributed as in the case of government agencies.

Persons. Estimated hire-purchase liability to companies. Liabilities to hire-purchase finance companies and to public corporations have been subtracted from total personal hire-purchase liabilities (Chapter 6, Table 31, item 3), and the balance has been distributed between public and private companies in proportion to their 'trade debtors'. No allowance has been made for debt to companies other than on hire-purchase.

Companies. 'Trade investments' (item 9) have been treated as liabilities of public companies and distributed between companies operating at home and abroad in proportion to their capital. 'Other liabilities' of public companies are trade debts obtained by distributing total 'trade creditors' items as described above. Public companies' holding of the liabilities of private companies are trade debts and 'unconsolidated subsidiaries' (item 11).

Banks. 'Cash' (item 16) has been distributed between Clearing and other banks in proportion to their total deposits.

Fixed assets. Include 'goodwill, &c.' (item 10).

External Sector, 'other liabilities'. This is the difference between 'trade and other debtors' (Table 36, item 13) and the credit they are assumed to have given to the domestic sector, i.e. to government trading agencies, public corporations, private companies, and to one another.

Private companies (Table 37). Items 7–12 are treated in the same way as for public companies. Item 13 is placed in the 'unidentified' line.

Co-operative societies (Table 38). Investments (item 8) have been distributed in accordance with figures provided by the Co-operative Union between quoted gilt-edged, local authority stocks, loans to persons, stocks and shares of public companies, and shares and deposits with building societies.

Item 7, 'Debtors' is treated as a liability of the personal sector, and 'cash' (item 9) is assumed to be held in balances with the Co-operative Wholesale Society Bank and is included in the 'other banks' line.

THE BANKING SYSTEM (Chapter 8)

Clearing and Scottish Banks

Figures in Table 39 have been adjusted for seasonal changes between December and March and for the estimated difference between the nominal and book value of investments. The figures, included with an opposite sign, in the 'adjustments' line are:

£ m.

	1953	*1954*	*1955*
Seasonal adjustments:			
Cash	−52	−30	−57
Call money	−72	−33	−60
Treasury bills	−227	−243	−350
Other bills	3	4	2
Advances	38	63	72
Investments	−26	−6	−72
Total seasonal	−336	−245	−465
Adjustment for nominal value of investments	125	77	143
Total	−211	−168	−322

The following notes indicate the allocation of items, where this is a matter of doubt.

Cash (item 4). Balances with the Bank of England are treated as the difference between 'cash' and 'notes and coin'.

Call-money (item 5). It is assumed that £50 m. is lent to the stock exchange (treated here as part of the personal sector) and the rest to the discount market.

Other bills (item 7). Acceptances outstanding on foreign account were given in 'Economic Trends', May 1958, as follows:

£ m. at end of year

1952	*1953*	*1954*
70	69	102

Hire-purchase bills were estimated as the difference between 'bank loans and bills' of the hire-purchase finance companies and the British Bankers' Association figure of hire purchase advances. This difference was:

£ m.

1953	*1954*	*1955*
22	29	29

These two items were allocated between Clearing and Scottish banks, other banks, and discount houses in proportion to their total government bill portfolios, and included in the 'hire purchase' and 'other foreign liabilities' lines. The remainder of the banks' bills have been placed among unidentified items.

Investments. British government and guaranteed securities (item 8*a*) were assumed to be 75 per cent. government stock with less than ten years to maturity. The remaining 25 per cent. was distributed between government securities and nationalization issues in proportion to the amount outstanding. Each category was then adjusted for nominal value on the assumption (not strictly accurate) that market and book values coincided. The resulting additions (appearing with a minus sign in the adjustment line) were:

	£ *m.*	
1953	*1954*	*1955*
125	77	143

'Other investments' (item 8*c*) are included with unidentified items. 'Subsidiaries and Trade Investments' (item 9) are included with 'unidentified items'.

Advances (item 10). Figures were taken from balance-sheets for public corporations (Chapter 3, Table II, item 2*a*), public companies (Chapter 7, Table 36, item 7*a*), private companies (Chapter 7, Table 37, item 3), building societies (Chapter 9, Table 48, item 3), and special financial institutions (Chapter 9, Table 51, item 3). 'Personal and Professional' advances and advances to agriculture and to stockbrokers in the British Bankers' Association Analysis were treated as liabilities of the personal sector. Figures for advances to local authorities, hire-purchase finance companies, and charities were also taken from the British Bankers' Association Analysis. All these items have been distributed between clearing banks and other banks in proportion to their total advances, and the balance has been included with unidentified items. The figures for the clearing banks were:

	£ *m.*	
1953	*1954*	*1955*
606	571	541

The fact that this unexplained balance is so large is due partly to the fact that we have been unable to make any specific allowance for advances to non-corporate business, other than agriculture and stockbroking, to finance and property companies, to British companies operating abroad, or to overseas companies. It also suggests, however, that we may have substantially underestimated the dependence of private companies on the banks.

Non-clearing Banks (Tables 40 and 41)

The treatment of the various items is the same as for clearing banks with two exceptions. No allowance is made for call money lent to the Stock Exchange; the deposits of the Birmingham Municipal Bank with the corporation are included in liabilities of local authorities and it is assumed that all other call-money is lent to the discount market. The whole of these banks' bills are assumed to be commercial bills, and these are distributed in the same way as the commercial bills of the clearing banks.

The Discount Market (Table 42)

Cash (item 4) is assumed to be held with the commercial banks. Bills (item 5*b*), other than Treasury bills, are treated in the same way as those of the banks. Treasury bills (item 5*a*) were adjusted for seasonal variation and investments (item 6) for estimated nominal value. The adjustments were:

£ *m.*

	1953	*1954*	*1955*
Treasury bills	−77	−42	−76
Government securities . . .	2	−2	9

NON-BANKING FINANCIAL INSTITUTIONS (Chapter 9)

Insurance companies (Table 45). British government securities (item 5) and nationalization issues (item 6), local authority stocks (item 7) and overseas government and municipal stocks were adjusted to nominal values. In adjusting government securities, the ratio used was that of nominal to market value of stocks longer than ten years. No adjustment was made to debentures and preference shares (items 9 and 10), where the difference between nominal and market values was small. Ordinary shares (item 12) were adjusted for market values on the assumption that the relationship between book values and market values was the same as that for the whole portfolio of the investment trusts (a separate estimate for investment trusts' ordinary shares was not possible). The result may, therefore, underestimate the market value of insurance companies' ordinary shares. Since fixed-interest stocks were at a discount, while ordinary shares were well above their nominal value, this involves substantial additions to the book value of assets. The amounts were as follows:

£ *m.*

	1953	*1954*	*1955*
Government securities . . .	149	91	106
Public corporations	71	50	66
Local authorities	15	10	14
Overseas stocks	48	29	39
Ordinary shares	19	209	444
Total	302	389	669

The shares of public companies were allocated between the various categories in proportion to the amounts outstanding, except that it was assumed that insurance companies did not hold the shares of other insurance companies.

Mortgages (item 12) and loans on policies (item 13) are treated as liabilities of the personal sector. We are informed that all local-authority obligations, whether securities or loans, are included in the category 'loans on the security of public rates' in the official returns. No doubt some mortgages were given to private companies, but it is impossible to separate these.

Agents' balances (item 15) and 'other assets' (item 17) in Chapter 9, Table 45, are entered here as unidentified items.

Pension funds (Table 46). The figures in the table were, for reasons indicated in the text, multiplied throughout by 2·5. Government and guaranteed stocks (item 1) were distributed between the central government and the public corporations in the proportion as shown by insurance companies. The following additions were made to adjust for nominal values:

£ *m.*

	1953	*1954*	*1955*
Government securities	61	35	42
Public corporations	24	18	26
Local authorities	12	8	13
Overseas stocks	6	4	6
Total	103	65	87

Mortgages are assumed to be those of local authorities. Debentures, preference, and ordinary shares (items 4, 5, and 6) distributed among British companies according to amounts outstanding.

Hire-purchase finance companies (Table 47). Hirers' balances are allocated 75 per cent. to persons and 25 per cent. to non-quoted companies. It is assumed that quoted companies are in a position to finance their purchases of equipment in less expensive ways. 'Liquid assets' (item 5) are assumed to be cash.

Building societies (Table 48). All mortgages (item 6) were assumed to be liabilities of the personal sector. Quoted investments (item 7*a*) were divided between government securities and those of public corporations in proportion to the amount outstanding. Unquoted investments (item 7*b*) were assumed, as indicated by our study of balance-sheets, to be local-authority mortgages. The adjustment for the nominal value of quoted securities was:

£ *m.*

	1953	*1954*	*1955*
Government	8	7	10
Public corporations	2	2	3
Total	10	9	13

Investment Trusts (Table 49). The estimated assets of unit trusts (£100 m. in 1953, £140 m. in 1954, and £180 m. in 1955) were added to ordinary shares (item 3*c*). Share portfolios were distributed among the various categories of public companies in proportion to total market values.

Finance and property companies (Table 50)

Investments (item 6) are distributed between various categories in the proportions shown by our study of balance-sheets analysed by the National Institute of Economic and Social Research.

Subsidiaries and trade investments (item 7) are treated as liabilities of unquoted companies.

Unidentified items consist of the unallocated balance of investments, 'other current assets' (item 9) and 'other assets' (item 10) of Table 50.

CHARITIES AND NON-PROFIT ORGANIZATIONS (Chapter 10)

In each case government securities, public corporation and local-authority stocks, and overseas securities were adjusted for nominal values. Where no direct evidence was available, shares of public companies were distributed among the various categories in proportion to the amounts outstanding. An adjustment for market value of ordinary shares was made for general charities and educational foundations. No adjustment was necessary for churches, as these estimates were compiled on a market-value basis. The total amount of these adjustments appears, for each category, in the adjustment line of the tables.

The allowance of £50 m. for the assets of miscellaneous organizations is assumed to consist of £10 m. each of quoted government securities, small savings securities, and commercial bank deposits, and £20 m. of savings-bank deposits.

UNALLOCATED ITEMS

In general, this is a residual representing the difference between total liabilities under each heading and the total appearing as assets of the sectors shown in preceding columns. Certain specific items (for which there seemed no other appropriate place) have, however, been included, and these are listed below.

Bank of England. 'Other deposits' (Chapter 2, Table 4, item 2*c*).

Public corporations, 'other liabilities' (Chapter 3, Table 13). 'Reserves' (item 1*e*); 'deferred liabilities and provisions' (item 3); interest and dividends due outside government (item 2*c*); balance of 'other capital liabilities' excluding savings deposits and pension rights (item 1*d*).

Local authorities (Chapter 4, Table 25). 'Reserves' (item 2*e*) and 'other special funds' (item 2*f*).

Public companies, 'other liabilities' (Chapter 7, Table 36). 'Minority interests' (item 6); 'interest and dividends due' (item 7*c*); 'provisions' (item 7*e*).

Private companies (Chapter 7, Table 37). 'Other liabilities' (item 6) and unidentified balance of capital and reserves (items 1 and 2).

Insurance companies (Chapter 9, Table 45). Estimated liabilities to foreigners for life assurance (item 2*a*). Insurance funds other than life (item 2*b*); outstanding claims (item 3); outstanding accounts, creditors, &c. (item 4).

Building societies (Chapter 9, Table 48). 'Reserves' (item 5) and 'other liabilities' (item 4).

Finance and Property (Chapter 9, Table 50). 'Mortgages' (item 2); 'current liabilities' (item 3); 'other liabilities' (item 4).

ADJUSTMENTS

These arise from differences in the method of valuation of the total liabilities shown in the final column and of the assets comprising those liabilities.

Bank of England. The difference between the figure at which the capital of the Bank stands in the Finance Accounts (Chapter 2, Table 2) and 'Capital' and 'Rest' in the Bank return (Table 4, item 1*a*).

Companies, ordinary shares, and reserves. The total is that of ordinary capital and reserves from Chapter 7, Table 36. Ordinary shares as assets are entered at estimated market value. Hence the 'unallocated' column shows the difference between our estimates of holdings by sector and the estimated total market values of Chapter 7, Table 34. The adjustment item is, therefore, the difference between this figure and that of Table 36.

Banks and financial companies. As in the case of public companies, the adjustment is the difference between the total of ordinary capital and reserves in the balance-sheets and the estimated market value of ordinary shares. Thus a positive sign indicates that the market value of ordinary shares is less than the book value of ordinary capital and reserves. For the clearing banks and Scottish banks the seasonal adjustment and net liabilities to subsidiaries are also included. These amounted to £374 m. in 1953, £383 m. in 1954, and £502 m. in 1955. For the discount market there is a seasonal adjustment to the value of Treasury bills amounting to £77 m. in 1953, £42 m. in 1954, and £76 m. in 1955.

TABLE 62. THE STRUCTURE OF

£ million

Liabilities of \ *Held by*					*Companies*			*Financial*		
	Central government	*Public corporations*	*Local authorities*	*Persons*	*Public companies*	*Private companies*	*Co-operative societies*	*Clearing and Scottish banks*	*Other banks*	*Discount houses*
Central government:										
Floating debt	1,850	9	..	..	5	2	..	980	..	638
Quoted securities	2,658	101	170	3,626	423	181	40	2,377	284	314
Other internal debt	1,546	..	19	3,021	213	91	..	..	..	..
External debt	..	..	..	..	..	..	..	..	..	..
Debt of trading agencies	..	..	..	..	70	30	..	..	..	..
Savings Bank deposits	..	..	..	2,722	..	..	..	..	..	..
Bank of England capital and deposits	104	..	..	..	..	..	..	244	25	..
Notes and coin	..	..	..	175	..	..	..	263	34	..
Public corporations:										
Securities and loans	1,244	..	..	744	..	..	..	119	14	..
Other liabilities	64	..	138	135	211	91	..	179	12	..
Local authorities:										
Securities and loans	2,232	6	227	316	..	..	18	19	74	..
Other liabilities	..	..	..	290	..	..	..	72	5	..
Persons	125	29	76	1,082	120	51	35	587	36	..
Non-financial companies:										
Public:										
Debentures and loans	1	11	..	289	14	..	..	..	..	..
Preference shares	..	34	..	777	38	..	1	..	..	..
Ordinary shares and reserves	..	232	..	2,968	144	..	3	..	..	..
Other liabilities	819	239	..	..	986	422	..	310	21	..
Private	350	103	..	1,942	459	181	..	133	9	..
Co-operative societies	..	..	..	329	..	..	..	..	..	..
Financial institutions:										
Clearing and Scottish banks:										
Capital and reserves	..	..	..	234	..	..	..	..	..	..
Deposits	..	56	19	2,096	843	362	..	..	..	11
Other banks	..	6	..	230	67	28	40	..	..	..
Discount houses	..	..	..	39	..	..	..	482	118	..
Insurance companies:										
Capital and reserves	..	..	..	88	..	..	..	..	..	..
Liability to policy-holders, &c.	..	..	..	2,448	..	..	..	..	..	..
Pension funds	..	..	..	995	..	..	..	..	..	..
H.P. finance companies	..	..	..	4	..	..	..	18	6	8
Building societies	..	..	..	1,531	..	..	10	2	..	..
Investments trusts	..	..	..	502	..	..	..	..	..	..
Finance and property companies	..	..	..	171	..	..	..	..	..	..
Trustee Savings Banks S.I. department	..	..	..	122	..	..	..	..	..	..
Other financial institutions	..	..	..	19	..	..	..	27	2	..
Charities	..	..	..	..	..	..	..	12	1	..
External sector:										
Foreign governments, &c.	297	..	..	429	..	..	..	25	10	..
British companies operating abroad—capital	80	30	..	902	44	..	..	..	..	..
Foreign companies—capital	207	13	..	539	..	..	..	..	..	..
Currency reserves	777	..	..	..	..	..	..	11	..	..
Other foreign liabilities	4	..	..	120	282	121	..	28	17	25
Real assets:										
Fixed capital	950	3,148	3,293	7,185	4,363	1,749	109	53	2	..
Stocks and work in progress	480	385	..	1,471	3,254	1,395	99	..	..	..
Unidentified items	14	168	35	1,223	44	259	6	710	107	39
Adjustments	−9	−10	−12	15	46	20	..	211	−15	75
TOTAL	13,793	4,560	3,965	38,779	11,626	4,983	361	6,863	762	1,110

PROPERTY OWNERSHIP, 1953

£ million

Institutions								Charities										
Insurance companies	*Pension funds*	*H.P. finance companies*	*Building societies*	*Investment trusts*	*Finance and property companies*	*Trustee Savings Banks S.I. department*	*Other financial institutions*	*Official trustee*	*Churches*	*Educational foundations*	*General charities*	*Friendly societies*	*Trade unions*	*Other charities*	*Foreign governments, &c.*	*Unallocated*	*Adjustments*	*Total*
..	..	..	..	..	..	..	2	..	..	..	..	..	..	..	..	1,227	..	4,713
909	365	..	84	..	19	44	3	91	84	154	294	158	26	30	..	1,497	..	13,932
..	..	..	..	..	..	..	..	2	5	..	..	..	..	11	3	412	..	5,323
..	..	..	..	..	..	..	..	..	..	..	..	..	..	..	3,007	12	..	3,020
..	..	..	..	..	..	..	..	..	..	..	..	..	..	..	..	..	..	100
..	..	..	..	..	..	..	..	..	..	..	..	2	..	20	..	8	..	2,752
..	..	..	..	..	..	..	..	..	..	..	..	..	..	..	..	75	−39	409
..	..	..	..	..	..	..	..	..	..	..	..	..	..	..	..	1,189	..	1,661
456	151	..	18	..	..	..	..	14	53	40	60	43	14	..	..	360	..	3,330
..	..	..	..	..	..	..	..	..	..	..	..	..	..	..	..	401	..	1,231
114	128	..	92	..	..	82	..	6	42	37	35	188	26	2	..	−151	..	3,493
..	..	..	..	..	..	..	..	..	..	..	..	..	..	..	..	103	..	470
404	..	72	1,396	..	..	..	24	..	..	..	..	1	..	..	..	..	..	4,038
189	52	..	..	26	..	..	56	1	3	4	13	..	..	..	..	142	..	801
199	63	..	..	41	..	..	9	2	7	2	14	..	..	1	..	−107	..	1,081
312	111	..	..	242	..	..	2	1	16	24	43	..	..	2	..	−160	2,439	6,379
..	..	..	..	..	..	..	..	..	..	..	..	..	..	..	..	568	..	3,365
..	..	23	..	..	11	..	21	..	..	..	..	..	..	..	..	1,751	..	4,983
..	..	..	..	..	..	..	..	..	..	..	..	..	..	..	..	33	..	362
18	7	..	..	14	..	..	..	..	2	1	2	..	..	..	..	104	−193	189
138	18	4	44	..	9	3	1	..	3	8	29	3	7	15	..	2,631	374	6,674
13	2	..	5	5	..	..	..	..	..	..	..	..	..	..	..	433	−67	762
3	1	..	..	2	..	..	..	..	..	..	..	..	..	..	..	422	43	1,110
..	2	..	..	5	..	..	..	..	..	..	1	..	..	..	..	3	203	302
..	..	..	..	..	..	..	..	..	..	..	..	..	..	..	..	1,060	..	3,507
..	..	..	..	..	..	..	..	..	..	..	..	..	..	..	..	..	..	995
1	..	..	..	..	..	..	..	..	..	..	..	..	..	..	..	69	..	106
..	..	..	..	..	..	..	..	..	..	..	..	..	..	..	..	100	..	1,643
116	35	..	..	..	..	..	..	..	2	2	3	..	..	..	..	−79	79	660
42	13	..	..	12	..	..	..	..	..	..	..	..	..	..	..	96	−22	312
..	..	..	..	..	..	..	..	..	..	..	..	..	..	..	..	9	..	131
13	3	..	..	2	..	..	..	..	..	..	..	..	..	..	..	54	..	120
..	..	..	..	..	..	..	..	..	..	..	..	..	..	..	..	2,101	..	2,114
417	54	..	..	..	..	..	..	3	8	7	10	18	5	2	..	−193	..	1,092
180	58	..	..	76	..	..	..	..	4	4	8	..	..	..	..	−226	..	1,160
70	..	..	..	235	..	..	..	..	..	..	..	..	..	..	..	6	..	1,070
..	..	..	..	..	..	..	..	..	..	..	..	..	..	..	..	..	..	788
..	..	..	..	..	..	..	..	..	..	..	..	..	..	..	..	..	..	597
257	17	..	..	..	226	..	..	..	102	194	109	45	3	31	..	..	..	21,836
..	..	..	..	..	..	..	..	..	..	..	..	..	..	..	..	..	..	7,084
260	16	7	12	..	47	2	3	..	8	8	25	7	2	4	..	..	..	3,006
−302	−103	..	−10	..	..	..	..	..	−21	−27	−46	−40	−8	..	..	..	..	−236
3,809	993	106	1,641	660	312	131	121	120	318	458	600	425	75	118	3,010	13,950	2,817	116,465

TABLE 63. THE STRUCTURE OF

£ million

Held by / Liabilities of					Companies			Financial		
	Central government	*Public corporations*	*Local authorities*	*Persons*	*Public companies*	*Private companies*	*Co-operative societies*	*Clearing and Scottish banks*	*Other banks*	*Discount houses*
Central government:										
Floating debt	1,699	10	..	..	4	2	..	1,010	..	588
Quoted securities	2,687	84	177	3,783	359	154	40	2,508	275	388
Other internal debt	1,557	..	18	2,985	269	115	..	..	..	..
External debt	..	..	..	..	..	..	..	..	..	..
Debt of trading agencies	..	..	..	..	72	31	..	..	..	..
Savings Bank deposits	..	..	..	2,708	..	..	..	..	..	..
Bank of England capital and deposits	90	..	..	..	..	..	..	236	27	..
Notes and coin	..	..	..	184	..	..	..	284	35	..
Public corporations:										
Securities and loans	1,319	..	..	741	..	..	..	116	15	..
Other liabilities	83	..	125	140	209	89	..	124	10	..
Local authorities:										
Securities and loans	2,512	9	247	283	..	..	18	25	87	..
Other liabilities	..	..	..	314	..	..	..	80	6	..
Persons	124	30	96	958	133	57	35	607	44	..
Non-financial companies:										
Public:										
Debentures and loans	1	15	..	283	12	..	..	..	..	..
Preference shares	..	21	..	762	32	..	1	..	..	..
Ordinary shares and reserves	..	187	..	3,755	160	..	3	..	..	..
Other liabilities	795	248	..	..	1,116	478	..	325	27	..
Private	341	106	..	1,878	511	205	..	140	11	..
Co-operative societies	..	..	..	331	..	..	..	..	..	..
Financial institutions:										
Clearing and Scottish banks:										
Capital and reserves	..	..	..	217	..	..	..	..	..	..
Deposits	..	53	21	2,180	843	362	..	..	..	12
Other banks	..	5	..	231	67	28	41	..	..	..
Discount houses	..	..	..	37	..	..	..	486	110	..
Insurance companies:										
Capital and reserves	..	..	..	82	..	..	..	..	..	..
Liabilities to policy-holders, &c.	..	..	..	2,619	..	..	..	..	..	..
Pension funds	..	..	..	1,182	..	..	..	..	..	..
H.P. finance companies	..	..	..	4	..	..	..	26	8	10
Building societies	..	..	..	1,747	..	..	10	2	..	..
Investment trusts	..	..	..	464	..	..	..	..	..	..
Finance and property companies	..	..	..	158	..	..	..	..	..	..
Trustee Savings Banks S.I. department	..	..	..	144	..	..	..	..	..	..
Other financial institutions	..	..	..	17	..	..	..	27	2	..
Charities	..	..	..	..	..	..	..	12	1	..
External sector:										
Foreign governments, &c.	380	..	..	385	..	..	..	33	11	..
British companies operating abroad—capital	125	30	..	1,106	47	..	..	..	..	..
Foreign companies—capital	247	19	..	618	..	..	..	..	..	..
Currency reserves	962	..	..	..	..	..	..	11	..	..
Other foreign liabilities	2	..	..	126	319	137	..	28	17	24
Real assets:										
Fixed capital	1,000	3,461	3,751	6,906	4,768	1,918	110	54	2	..
Stocks and work in progress	435	353	..	1,523	3.512	1,505	100	..	..	..
Unidentified items	17	136	38	925	38	264	6	681	118	64
Adjustments	−77	−5	−6	279	61	26	..	268	−8	44
TOTAL	14,299	4,762	4,467	40,055	12,532	5,371	364	7,083	798	1,130

PROPERTY OWNERSHIP, 1954

£ million

Institutions								*Charities*										
Insurance companies	*Pension funds*	*H.P. finance companies*	*Building societies*	*Investment trusts*	*Finance and property companies*	*Trustee Savings Banks S.I. department*	*Other financial institutions*	*Official trustee*	*Churches*	*Educational foundations*	*General charities*	*Friendly societies*	*Trade unions*	*Other charities*	*Foreign governments, &c.*	*Unallocated*	*Adjustments*	*Total*
..	..	..	..	..	..	..	2	..	..	..	..	..	..	..	..	1,504	..	4,819
849	326	..	99	..	19	42	3	94	77	148	283	157	24	30	..	1,914	..	14,520
..	..	..	..	..	..	..	..	2	4	..	..	..	..	11	3	332	..	5,296
..	..	..	..	..	..	..	..	..	..	..	..	..	..	..	2,893	11	..	2,904
..	..	..	..	..	..	..	..	..	..	..	..	..	..	..	..	..	..	103
..	..	..	..	..	..	..	..	..	..	..	..	2	..	20	..	8	..	2,738
..	..	..	..	..	..	..	..	..	..	..	..	..	..	..	..	73	−39	386
..	..	..	..	..	..	..	..	..	..	..	..	..	..	..	..	1,233	..	1,736
504	192	..	20	..	..	..	..	14	46	38	57	41	13	..	..	484	..	3,600
..	..	..	..	..	..	..	..	..	..	..	..	..	..	..	..	381	..	1,161
109	138	..	110	..	..	103	..	6	40	36	33	190	24	2	..	−21	..	3,951
..	..	..	..	..	..	..	..	..	..	..	..	..	..	..	..	115	..	515
442	..	98	1,574	..	..	..	26	..	..	..	..	1	..	..	..	..	..	4,225
208	64	..	..	29	..	..	52	1	3	4	13	..	..	..	..	242	..	927
211	71	..	..	47	..	..	8	2	6	2	14	..	..	1	..	−45	..	1,133
466	171	..	..	337	..	..	3	2	22	20	57	..	..	2	..	206	1,471	6,862
..	..	..	..	..	..	..	..	..	..	..	..	..	..	..	..	622	..	3,611
..	..	32	..	..	10	..	23	..	..	..	..	..	..	..	..	2,114	..	5,371
..	..	..	..	..	..	..	..	..	..	..	..	..	..	..	..	35	..	366
28	10	..	..	19	..	..	..	..	2	2	3	..	..	..	..	30	−114	197
135	22	6	53	..	3	5	1	..	3	8	29	4	6	15	..	2,742	383	6,886
15	3	..	5	7	..	..	..	..	..	..	1	..	..	..	..	436	−40	799
5	2	..	..	3	..	..	..	..	..	..	..	..	..	..	..	465	22	1,130
..	4	..	..	7	..	..	..	..	..	..	2	..	..	..	..	22	202	319
..	..	..	..	..	..	..	..	..	..	..	..	..	..	..	..	1,149	..	3,768
..	..	..	..	..	..	..	..	..	..	..	..	..	..	..	..	..	..	1,182
..	..	..	..	..	..	..	..	..	..	..	..	..	..	..	..	98	..	146
..	..	..	..	..	..	..	..	..	..	..	..	..	..	..	..	108	..	1,867
139	45	..	..	..	..	..	..	..	2	2	5	..	..	..	..	149	78	884
47	15	..	..	16	..	..	..	..	..	..	..	..	..	..	..	144	−42	338
..	..	..	..	..	..	..	..	..	..	..	..	..	..	..	..	8	..	152
13	4	..	..	2	..	..	..	..	..	..	..	..	..	..	..	55	..	120
..	..	..	..	..	..	..	..	..	..	..	..	..	..	..	..	2,116	..	2,129
415	60	..	..	..	..	..	..	3	6	7	10	18	5	2	..	−165	..	1,170
231	78	..	..	101	..	..	..	..	5	6	10	..	..	..	..	−184	..	1,555
102	..	..	..	316	..	..	..	..	..	..	..	..	..	..	..	64	..	1,366
..	..	..	..	..	..	..	..	..	..	..	..	..	..	..	..	..	..	973
..	..	..	..	..	..	..	..	..	..	..	..	..	..	..	..	..	..	653
286	22	..	..	..	254	..	..	..	104	194	109	47	3	31	..	..	..	23,020
..	..	..	..	..	..	..	..	..	..	..	..	..	..	..	..	..	..	7,428
271	20	10	13	..	52	2	3	..	8	8	25	7	2	4	..	..	..	2,712
−389	−65	..	−9	..	..	..	..	..	−12	−17	−15	−26	−5	..	..	..	..	8
4,087	1,182	146	1,865	884	338	152	121	124	316	458	600	441	72	118	2,896	16,445	1,921	123,026

TABLE 64. THE STRUCTURE OF

£ million

Held by / *Liabilities of*					*Companies*			*Financial*		
	Central government	*Public corporations*	*Local authorities*	*Persons*	*Public companies*	*Private companies*	*Co-operative societies*	*Clearing and Scottish banks*	*Other banks*	*Discount houses*
Central government:										
Floating debt	2,057	1	..	..	7	3	..	860	..	554
Quoted securities	2,718	155	191	3,769	502	215	39	2,575	286	406
Other internal debt	1,597	..	16	3,010	233	100	..	..	..	..
External debt	..	..	..	..	..	..	..	..	..	..
Debt of trading agencies	..	..	..	..	29	13	..	..	..	..
Savings Bank deposits	..	..	..	2,740	..	..	..	..	..	..
Bank of England capital and deposits	74	..	..	..	..	..	..	248	28	..
Notes and coin	..	..	..	195	..	..	..	272	34	..
Public corporations:										
Securities and loans	1,484	..	..	773	..	..	..	124	14	..
Other liabilities	71	..	112	144	242	103	..	180	14	..
Local authorities										
Securities and loans	2,842	20	261	286	..	..	18	28	95	..
Other liabilities	..	..	..	340	..	..	..	96	7	..
Persons	151	31	131	925	153	66	38	641	44	..
Non-financial companies:										
Public:										
Debentures and loans	1	14	..	281	11	..	..	..	..	..
Preference shares	..	20	..	649	26	..	1	..	..	..
Ordinary shares and reserves	..	178	..	4,401	179	..	3	..	..	..
Other liabilities	814	269	..	..	1,340	574	..	395	32	..
Private	348	116	..	1,875	608	246	..	169	14	..
Co-operative societies	..	..	..	339	..	..	..	..	..	..
Financial institutions:										
Clearing and Scottish banks:										
Capital and reserves	..	..	..	226	..	..	..	..	..	..
Deposits	..	52	21	2,270	730	311	..	..	..	12
Other banks	..	6	..	239	55	25	45	..	..	..
Discount houses	..	..	..	39	..	..	..	458	137	..
Insurance companies:										
Capital and reserves	..	..	..	151	..	..	..	..	..	..
Liabilities to policy-holders, &c.	..	..	..	2,838	..	..	..	..	..	..
Pension funds	..	..	..	1,366	..	..	..	..	..	..
H.P. finance companies	..	..	..	9	..	..	..	48	9	11
Building societies	..	..	..	1,939	..	..	10	2	..	..
Investment trusts	..	..	..	522	..	..	..	..	..	..
Finance and property companies	..	..	..	172	..	..	..	..	..	..
Trustee Savings Banks S.I. department	..	..	..	193	..	..	..	..	..	..
Other financial institutions	..	..	..	15	..	..	..	27	2	..
Charities	..	..	..	..	..	..	..	13	1	..
External sector:										
Foreign governments, &c.	375	..	..	336	..	..	..	40	13	..
British companies operating abroad—capital	210	25	..	1,358	55	..	..	..	..	..
Foreign companies—capital	316	21	..	730	..	..	..	..	..	..
Currency reserves	956	..	..	..	..	..	..	11	..	..
Other foreign liabilities	1	..	..	135	340	146	..	43	22	37
Real assets:										
Fixed capital	1,079	3,779	4,171	7,155	5,547	2,250	115	56	2	..
Stocks and work in progress	244	300	..	1,596	3,944	1,690	103	..	..	..
Unidentified items	16	166	41	1,087	67	287	4	677	125	83
Adjustments	−131	−14	−13	127	31	13	..	322	−16	67
TOTAL	15,223	5,139	4,931	42,230	14,099	6,042	376	7,285	863	1,170

PROPERTY OWNERSHIP, 1955

£ million

Institutions								*Charities*										
Insurance companies	*Pension funds*	*H.P. finance companies*	*Building societies*	*Investment trusts*	*Finance and property companies*	*Trustee Savings Banks S.I. department*	*Other financial institutions*	*Official trustee*	*Churches*	*Educational foundations*	*General charities*	*Friendly societies*	*Trade unions*	*Other charities*	*Foreign governments, &c.*	*Unallocated*	*Adjustments*	*Total*
..	..	..	..	..	..	..	..	..	..	..	..	..	..	..	..	1,765	..	5,247
872	347	..	110	..	19	45	3	97	76	151	289	166	23	30	..	1,488	..	14,572
..	..	..	..	..	..	..	..	2	4	..	..	..	..	11	3	340	..	5,316
..	..	..	..	..	..	..	..	..	..	..	..	..	..	..	2,728	8	..	2,736
..	..	..	..	..	..	..	..	..	..	..	..	..	..	..	..	..	..	42
..	..	..	..	..	..	..	..	..	..	..	..	2	..	20	..	8	..	2,770
..	..	..	..	..	..	..	..	..	..	..	..	..	..	..	..	65	−39	376
..	..	..	..	..	..	..	..	..	..	..	..	..	..	..	..	1,357	..	1,858
547	218	..	23	..	..	..	..	15	44	39	58	44	13	..	..	444	..	3,840
..	..	..	..	..	..	..	..	..	..	..	..	..	..	..	..	433	..	1,299
116	156	..	120	..	..	146	..	6	43	37	34	201	23	2	..	−72	..	4,362
..	..	..	..	..	..	..	..	..	..	..	..	..	..	..	..	125	..	568
479	..	152	1,752	..	..	..	26	..	..	..	..	1	..	..	..	..	..	4,590
259	80	..	..	29	..	..	53	1	3	4	13	..	..	..	..	264	..	1,013
235	76	..	..	44	..	..	9	2	6	2	14	..	..	1	..	93	..	1,178
675	223	..	..	471	..	..	2	2	37	23	68	..	..	2	..	1,019	531	7,814
..	..	..	..	..	..	..	..	..	..	..	..	..	..	..	..	670	..	4,094
..	..	51	..	..	9	..	18	..	..	..	..	..	..	..	..	2,588	..	6,042
..	..	..	..	..	..	..	..	..	..	..	..	..	..	..	..	37	..	376
35	11	..	..	24	..	..	..	..	2	1	3	..	..	..	..	73	−169	206
126	25	8	53	..	4	7	1	..	3	8	29	4	6	15	..	2,892	502	7,079
18	4	..	6	9	..	..	..	..	1	..	1	..	..	..	..	513	−60	862
6	2	..	..	4	..	..	..	..	..	..	..	..	..	..	..	476	48	1,170
..	8	..	..	16	..	..	..	..	..	1	2	..	..	..	..	72	113	363
..	..	..	..	..	..	..	..	..	..	..	..	..	..	..	..	1,236	..	4,074
..	..	..	..	..	..	..	..	..	..	..	..	..	..	..	..	..	..	1,366
2	..	..	..	..	..	..	..	..	..	..	..	..	..	..	..	147	..	226
..	..	..	..	..	..	..	..	..	..	..	..	..	..	..	..	115	..	2,066
183	59	..	..	..	..	..	..	..	4	2	7	..	..	..	..	266	141	1,184
56	19	..	..	19	..	..	..	..	..	..	..	..	..	..	..	179	−76	369
..	..	..	..	..	..	..	..	..	..	..	..	..	..	..	..	9	..	202
13	4	..	..	2	..	..	..	..	..	..	..	..	..	..	..	53	..	116
..	..	..	..	..	..	..	..	..	..	..	..	..	..	..	..	2,153	..	2,167
441	70	..	..	..	..	..	..	3	5	7	10	19	5	2	..	−177	..	1,149
307	99	..	..	144	..	..	..	..	7	4	15	..	..	..	..	−89	..	2,135
134	..	..	..	422	..	..	..	..	..	..	..	..	..	..	..	−6	..	1,617
..	..	..	..	..	..	..	..	..	..	..	..	..	..	..	..	..	..	967
..	..	..	..	..	..	..	..	..	..	..	..	..	..	..	..	..	..	724
312	28	..	..	..	281	..	..	..	107	194	109	50	3	31	..	..	..	25,269
..	..	..	..	..	..	..	..	..	..	..	..	..	..	..	..	..	..	7,877
290	24	15	14	..	56	3	3	..	7	8	25	8	2	4	..	..	..	3,012
−669	−87	..	−13	..	..	..	..	..	−15	−22	−75	−34	−6	..	..	..	..	−535
4,437	1,366	226	2,066	1,184	369	202	116	128	334	459	600	461	68	118	2,731	18,544	991	131,758

TABLE 65. THE STRUCTURE OF

£ million

Liabilities of / *Held by*					*Companies*			*Financial*		
	Central government	*Public corporations*	*Local authorities*	*Persons*	*Public companies*	*Private companies*	*Co-operative societies*	*Clearing and Scottish banks*	*Other banks*	*Discount houses*
Central government:										
Floating debt	1,869	7	..	..	5	2	..	950	..	593
Quoted securities	2,688	113	179	3,726	428	183	40	2,487	282	369
Other internal debt	1,567	..	18	3,005	238	102	..	..	..	..
External debt	..	..	..	..	..	..	..	..	..	..
Debt of trading agencies	..	..	..	..	57	25	..	..	..	..
Savings Bank deposits	..	..	..	2,723	..	..	..	..	..	..
Bank of England capital and deposits	89	..	..	..	..	..	..	243	27	..
Notes and coin	..	..	..	185	..	..	..	273	34	..
Public corporations:										
Securities and loans	1,349	..	..	753	..	..	..	120	14	..
Other liabilities	73	..	125	140	221	94	..	161	12	..
Local authorities:										
Securities and loans	2,529	12	245	295	..	..	18	24	85	..
Other liabilities	..	..	..	315	..	..	..	83	6	..
Persons	133	30	101	988	135	58	36	612	41	..
Non-financial companies:										
Public:										
Debentures and loans	1	13	..	284	12	..	..	..	..	..
Preference shares	..	25	..	729	32	..	1	..	..	..
Ordinary shares and reserves	..	199	..	3,708	161	..	3	..	..	..
Other liabilities	809	252	..	..	1,147	491	..	343	27	..
Private	346	108	..	1,898	526	211	..	147	11	..
Co-operative societies	..	..	..	333	..	..	..	..	..	..
Financial institutions:										
Clearing and Scottish banks:										
Capital and reserves	..	..	..	226	..	..	..	..	..	..
Deposits	..	54	20	2,182	805	345	..	..	..	12
Other banks	..	6	..	233	63	27	42	..	..	..
Discount houses	..	..	..	38	..	..	..	475	122	..
Insurance companies:										
Capital and reserves	..	..	..	107	..	..	..	..	..	..
Liabilities to policy-holders, &c.	..	..	..	2,635	..	..	..	..	..	..
Pension funds	..	..	..	1,181	..	..	..	..	..	..
H.P. finance companies	..	..	..	6	..	..	..	31	8	10
Building societies	..	..	..	1,739	..	..	10	2	..	..
Investment trusts	..	..	..	496	..	..	..	..	..	..
Finance and property companies	..	..	..	167	..	..	..	..	..	..
Trustee Savings Banks S.I. department	..	..	..	153	..	..	..	..	..	..
Other financial institutions	..	..	..	17	..	..	..	27	2	..
Charities	..	..	..	..	..	..	..	12	1	..
External sector:										
Foreign governments, &c.	351	..	..	383	..	..	..	33	11	..
British companies operating abroad—capital	138	28	..	1,122	49	..	..	..	..	..
Foreign companies—capital	257	18	..	629	..	..	..	..	..	..
Currency reserves	898	..	..	..	..	..	..	11	..	..
Other foreign liabilities	2	..	..	127	314	135	..	33	19	29
Real assets:										
Fixed capital	1,010	3,463	3,738	7,082	4,893	1,972	111	54	2	..
Stocks and work in progress	386	346	..	1,530	3,570	1,530	101	..	..	..
Unidentified items	16	157	38	1,078	50	270	5	689	117	62
Adjustments	−72	−10	−10	140	46	20	..	267	−13	62
TOTAL	14,438	4,820	4,454	40,355	12,752	5,465	367	7,077	808	1,137

PROPERTY OWNERSHIP, AVERAGE 1953–5

£ million

Institutions								*Charities*										
Insurance companies	*Pension funds*	*H.P. finance companies*	*Building societies*	*Investment trusts*	*Finance and property companies*	*Trustee Savings Banks S.I. department*	*Other financial institutions*	*Official trustee*	*Churches*	*Educational foundations*	*General charities*	*Friendly societies*	*Trade unions*	*Other charities*	*Foreign government, &c.*	*Unallocated*	*Adjustments*	*Total*
..	..	..	..	..	..	..	1	..	..	..	..	..	..	..	..	1,499	..	4,926
877	346	..	98	..	19	44	3	94	79	151	289	160	24	30	..	1,633	..	14,341
..	..	..	..	..	..	..	..	2	4	..	..	..	..	11	3	361	..	5,312
..	..	..	..	..	..	..	..	..	..	..	..	..	..	..	2,876	10	..	2,887
..	..	..	..	..	..	..	..	..	..	..	..	..	..	..	..	..	..	82
..	..	..	..	..	..	..	..	..	..	..	..	2	..	20	..	8	..	2,753
..	..	..	..	..	..	..	..	..	..	..	..	..	..	..	..	71	−39	390
..	..	..	..	..	..	..	..	..	..	..	..	..	..	..	..	1,260	..	1,752
502	187	..	20	..	..	..	..	14	48	39	58	43	13	..	..	429	..	3,590
..	..	..	..	..	..	..	..	..	..	..	..	..	..	..	..	405	..	1,230
113	141	..	107	..	..	110	..	6	42	37	34	193	24	2	..	−81	..	3,935
..	..	..	..	..	..	..	..	..	..	..	..	..	..	..	..	114	..	518
442	..	107	1,574	..	..	..	25	..	..	..	..	1	..	..	..	..	..	4,284
219	66	..	..	28	..	..	54	1	3	4	13	..	..	..	..	216	..	914
215	70	..	..	44	..	..	9	2	6	2	14	..	..	1	..	−20	..	1,131
484	168	..	..	350	..	..	2	2	25	22	56	..	..	2	..	355	1,480	7,018
..	..	..	..	..	..	..	..	..	..	..	..	..	..	..	..	620	..	3,690
..	..	35	..	..	10	..	21	..	..	..	..	..	..	..	..	2,151	..	5,465
..	..	..	..	..	..	..	..	..	..	..	..	..	..	..	..	35	..	368
27	9	..	..	19	..	..	..	..	2	1	3	..	..	..	..	69	−159	197
133	22	6	50	..	5	5	1	..	3	8	29	4	6	15	..	2,755	420	6,880
15	3	..	5	7	..	..	..	..	..	..	1	..	..	..	..	461	−56	808
5	2	..	..	3	..	..	..	..	..	..	..	..	..	..	..	454	38	1,137
..	5	..	..	9	..	..	..	..	..	..	2	..	..	..	..	32	173	328
..	..	..	..	..	..	..	..	..	..	..	..	..	..	..	..	1,148	..	3,783
..	..	..	..	..	..	..	..	..	..	..	..	..	..	..	..	..	..	1,181
1	..	..	..	..	..	..	..	..	..	..	..	..	..	..	..	105	..	159
..	..	..	..	..	..	..	..	..	..	..	..	..	..	..	..	108	..	1,859
146	46	..	..	..	..	..	..	..	3	2	5	..	..	..	..	112	99	909
48	16	..	..	16	..	..	..	..	..	..	..	..	..	..	..	140	−47	340
..	..	..	..	..	..	..	..	..	..	..	..	..	..	..	..	8	..	162
13	4	..	..	2	..	..	..	..	..	..	..	..	..	..	..	54	..	119
..	..	..	..	..	..	..	..	..	..	..	..	..	..	..	..	2,123	..	2,137
424	61	..	..	..	..	..	..	3	6	7	10	18	5	2	..	−178	..	1,137
239	78	..	..	107	..	..	..	..	5	5	11	..	..	..	..	−166	..	1,617
102	..	..	..	324	..	..	..	..	..	..	..	..	..	..	..	21	..	1,351
..	..	..	..	..	..	..	..	..	..	..	..	..	..	..	..	..	..	909
..	..	..	..	..	..	..	..	..	..	..	..	..	..	..	..	..	..	658
285	22	..	..	..	254	..	..	..	104	194	109	47	3	31	..	..	..	23,375
..	..	..	..	..	..	..	..	..	..	..	..	..	..	..	..	..	..	7,463
274	20	11	13	..	52	2	3	..	8	8	25	7	2	4	..	..	..	2,910
−453	−85	..	−11	..	..	..	..	..	−16	−22	−57	−33	−6	..	..	..	..	−254
4,111	1,180	159	1,857	909	340	162	119	124	323	458	600	442	72	118	2,879	16,313	1,910	123,750

13

CONCLUSIONS

WE are now in a position to relate our results to the concepts of capital and wealth discussed in Chapter 1. The best starting-point for this is probably Table 65, which gives the averages of our estimates for the three years 1953–5.

The stock of fixed assets, on our method of valuation, was £23,375 m. and the value of stocks £7,463 m. making a total of £30,838 m. Real assets were valued mainly on the basis of book values and valuation on a replacement-cost basis would, as indicated in the previous chapter, have raised their value very substantially; fixed assets alone would then have been around £33,000 m. If, on the other hand, we had taken the market value of company shares as the measure of the value of their assets, we should have reached a figure lower than that obtained from book values.

In order to estimate national wealth, in the sense of assets owned by British residents, we add to the estimate of national capital the monetary gold stock, the assets of British companies operating abroad, and financial claims on non-residents, and deduct the value of property held by and debts due to non-residents. Overseas assets were valued in Table 65 at £5,672 m. If the Bank of England estimates of ordinary shares are revalued at market value (Chap. 11, p. 144) the total is raised to about £6,600 m. On the other hand, overseas liabilities were estimated in Chapter 11 at around £9,000 m., so that national wealth, on our basis of valuation, would be about £28,400 m.

Private net worth differs from national wealth in excluding the real assets and overseas financial assets of the public sector and including the net financial claims of the private sector or the public sector. Since the latter were much larger than the former, private net worth is, of course, much greater than national wealth. The public sector had fixed assets and stocks (Table 65) of over

£8,900 m. and financial claims on the overseas sector (including the gold reserve of nearly £1,700 m.). On the other hand, the central government had £26,000 m. of liabilities held outside the public sector (including the note issue and savings-bank deposits) and local authorities and public corporations had liabilities to the private and overseas sectors combined of over £4,900 m. The total net financial liability of the public sector was thus nearly £31,000 m. On the basis of the rather slender evidence of Chapter 11, it seems likely that about £6,000 m. of this was due to the overseas sector, and about £25,000 m. to the domestic private sector. Against this, the public sector had £2,100 m. of claims on the private sector. In round figures, therefore, our estimate of private net worth would be:

		£ m.
	National wealth . . .	28,500
less	Public sectors' holding. .	10,600
		17,900
plus	Private sectors' net financial claims on public sector .	22,900
		40,800

The only net asset holders in the private sector are persons and charities since companies and other institutions all have liabilities equal to their assets, so that they cancel out when their accounts are consolidated. Hence if all items had been identified and correctly assigned to the various sectors, and if the basis of valuation had been entirely consistent, our estimate of private net worth would have equalled the total net assets of persons and charities. The gross assets of persons in Table 65 were £40,267 m., and their liabilities (on the basis of Chap. 6, p. 72) were £4,283 m. The net assets of charities were £2,124 m., so that by this calculation private net worth comes out at only £38,100 m.

The discrepancy is due to a number of differences in valuation and to the treatment of unidentified items. The main ones are as follows:

1. In the estimate of national wealth we took the value of overseas holdings from Chapter 11 instead of from Table 65,

and this raised the figure for national wealth and so the first estimate of private net worth.

2. In computing national wealth the assets of companies were taken at book value. Personal holdings of ordinary shares were taken at market value which was less than the book value of the assets 'belonging' to shareholders.

3. In our first estimate of net worth we took a figure for overseas liabilities of the public sector based on Chapter 11, which was rather larger than the unidentified public sector liabilities of Table 65. This would tend to make our first estimate lower than the second.

4. This, however, is more than outweighed by other unidentified items. Some of these represent overseas holdings and many are of a kind that would cancel out on consolidation. Some, however, represent items which should form part of private net worth. The most important of these is cash, the problem of which was discussed in Chapter 12. In our first estimate of private net worth, public sector securities held by the banks were treated as assets of the private sector, yet much of the cash which forms the counterpart of these securities was unidentified, and does not therefore figure in the second estimate.

In view of the many uncertainties involved the discrepancy of just under 7 per cent. between the two figures does not seem unduly large. It seems likely, however, that the higher figure is more nearly correct.

The most striking feature about private net worth is that well over half of it is composed of claims on the public sector, the vast majority of which are not the counterpart of any real assets.

The concept of private gross worth, as explained in Chapter 1, is of very limited usefulness, but may be worth a brief glance. The gross worth of the private sector from Table 65 is £82,000 m. or just over double the net worth. When a person or a charitable organization is the direct owner either of a real asset or of a claim on the public or overseas sectors, this appears only once in the table, and gives rise to no discrepancy between gross and net worth. Such direct ownership still accounts for rather more than half of private net worth. The discrepancy between net and gross worth arises when a person or charity owns the liability of an institution which owns (directly or at a farther remove) a real asset or a claim on the public or overseas sector. If, for example, a person holds a life-assurance policy, and the insurance company has shares in an investment trust which has shares in companies which own real assets, the value of the policy would occur four times—as a net asset of the person and as an asset with a corresponding liability in the accounts of each of the institutions. For those assets which are not directly owned, the ratio of gross to net worth is over four to one, so that on an average more than three intermediaries are interposed between the original asset and the ultimate beneficiary. This is a rather surprisingly high figure, and is some indication of the complexities of the modern capital market.

It would have been very desirable to have been able to compare our present estimates of capital and wealth with those of earlier writers and so, in Sir Robert Giffen's words, to 'take stock of national progress'. Unfortunately twenty years of inflation have so distorted values that such a comparison would contain too big a margin of error to be useful. There are other comparisons, however, between the different sectors of our present study, and of the types of property held by each where the problem of valuation is less formidable, and which throw some light on our present position.

One of these is the distribution of fixed assets between sectors. The division of fixed assets between the main sectors, from Table 65, was:

	£ m.	£ m.	%
Central government . .	1,010		4·3
Public corporations . .	3,463		14·8
Local authorities. . .	3,738		16·0
Total public sector . .		8,211	35·1
Persons	7,082		30·3
Non-financial companies .	6,976		29·9
Financial companies . .	617		2·6
Charities	488		2·1
Total private sector . .		15,163	64·9
Total		23,374	

Rather more than a third of all fixed capital is now owned by public agencies. The most important items are the telegraph and telephone systems and the other fixed assets of the Post Office; the capital of the nationalized coal, gas, electricity, and transport industries; and the houses built by local authorities. Clearly, nationalization, a high level of investment by the public corporations and a large amount of local authority housebuilding, has raised the proportion of fixed assets in the public sector very substantially since the war. It has not, however, increased the net assets of the public sector to nearly the same extent. Only a small part of new investment has been financed out of the revenue of the investing institutions themselves. A considerably larger part has been provided out of the savings of other public agencies, chiefly the central government and—in the earlier post-war years—the national insurance funds. A larger part still, however, has come from the taking over of assets from the private sector on nationalization and from new investment financed by borrowing from the private sector. The effect of this has been to place the legal ownership (and hence the control) of the fixed assets in the hands of the public agency concerned and to substitute a financial claim on the public sector for one on the private sector. Since the claims on the public sector carry a fixed interest and a government guarantee, whereas those on firms in the private sector are largely equity, this process has had an important effect on the composition of financial assets, of which more later.

It is interesting to note that persons still own around 30 per cent. of all fixed assets, about the same proportion as companies. This statement, however, requires two qualifications. The estimate of personal property is derived from its assessment for death duty (based on market value), whereas that of public authorities and companies is based on book values; the proportion of personal property is, therefore, likely to be somewhat exaggerated. A large part of personal property consists, of course, of houses; the estate-duty figures do not separate houses from other buildings but, on the average of 1953–5, we estimate the total value of buildings held by persons at £5,145 m. or

72 per cent. of all personal real assets. Our estimates thus confirm the generally held view that industrial fixed assets owned directly by persons are now very small, and that this type of capital is overwhelmingly in the hands of either the company or the public sectors.

Real assets now form only about 17 per cent. of all personal property, and the rest consists of financial claims of one kind or another. Of these over £11,000 m., representing more than a quarter of all personal property, are direct claims on the public sector. Our estimates from Table 65 are:

	£ *m.*
Quoted national debt	3,726
'Small savings' securities and post-war credits	3,005
P.O. and Trustee Savings Bank deposits	2,723
Notes and coin	185
Public corporations' liabilities	893
Local authorities' liabilities	610
	11,142

This, of course, takes no account of the further large volume of personal assets in the form of bank deposits, insurance policies, and pension rights that are largely backed by government securities in the hands of financial intermediaries.

This is only one aspect of the tremendous growth of the public debt as a result of two world wars and the move towards public ownership. Besides personal holders, the debt has now come to form an important part of the assets of most financial institutions. In considering the distribution of the quoted debt, it is best to take quoted government securities and nationalization stocks together, as the market makes no distinction between them provided that they are of similar date. Local-authority stocks, on the other hand, are distinct in several ways: they do not carry a central government guarantee, the amounts of issues are smaller, the market is narrower, and the distribution among varous types of holder is very different from that of government stock.

For the three years 1953–5 the amount of the quoted securities of the central government and the public corporations averaged over £17,000 m., and we estimate that it was distributed as follows:

	£ m.	%
Public agencies	3,555	20·7
Persons.	4,479	26·1
Non-financial companies .	651	3·8
Banks and discount houses .	3,272	19·1
Insurance companies . .	1,379	8·0
Pension funds . . .	533	3·1
Other financial companies .	140	0·8
Charities	1,042	6·1
Unidentified	2,090	12·2
	17,141	100·0

For reasons indicated in Chapters 6 and 7 the estimate of personal holdings may be too high while that for companies may understate their holding of Treasury bills and overstate their holding of gilt-edged. The amount of quoted securities held overseas is, therefore, probably rather greater than the £2,090 m. which were unidentified in our estimates.

Looking at the matter in another way, we may consider the importance of public sector liabilities in the assets of different parts of the private sector. Here it is relevant to consider not only quoted securities, but all public sector liabilities. This has already been done for persons; non-financial companies naturally hold only comparatively small amounts, but for all the main types of financial institution claims on the public sector are a large part of total assets. The banks held over half their assets in Treasury bills, quoted securities of, and advances to, the public sector. If we also count their cash and the large proportion of their call-money which is used to hold Treasury bills or short-dated government stock, the proportion of their assets directly or indirectly based on public sector liabilities rises to over two-thirds. The discount houses had about 85 per cent., insurance companies 35 per cent., pension funds 45 per cent., and charities 50 per cent. of their assets in claims on the public sector.

The growth of public debt is not the only way in which financial claims have been multiplied in the modern world. The concentration of industrial fixed assets in the hands of companies; the finance of private housebuilding through building societies and (to a lesser extent) insurance companies; and the growth of hire-purchase have all had a similar effect.

Along with the growth of financial claims has gone the growth of financial intermediaries. Financial intermediaries are of many kinds as is apparent from Chapters 8 and 9, but their common characteristic is that they all create additional links in the chain of ownership between the real asset or other constituent of private net worth and the ultimate beneficiary. They each perform a specialized service or group of services, and each also makes a general contribution to the smooth working of the capital market in such ways as providing expert investment knowledge and helping to provide a wide and active market in the type of assets which they hold.

An important general consequence of the growth of financial assets and the rise of financial intermediaries is its effect on liquidity. Some institutions, such as the banks, have a conventional division between 'liquid' and 'illiquid' assets and the problem is often discussed in terms of such a sharp line. In reality, however, different assets all have varying degrees of liquidity and one can move in a series of very small steps from the perfectly liquid to the very illiquid. A full treatment of the question of liquidity thus involves consideration of the whole structure of property ownership.

Clearly much of the public debt is highly liquid; not only can the floating debt, savings-bank deposits, and small savings securities be converted into cash quickly and with little or no loss, but a large part of the quoted debt is so near to maturity that it is subject to only minor fluctuations in price. The growth of financial claims on the private sector and the development of organized markets in them also adds to liquidity; the share of a joint-stock company is a more liquid asset than a piece of industrial plant. Frequently, too, the growth of financial intermediaries increases liquidity still further; a deposit with a building society or a hire-purchase company is much more liquid than a personal IOU. This is not always the case (a life-assurance policy, for example, is not a very liquid asset) but it is probably true of most claims on financial intermediaries.

The most striking manifestation of the growth of liquidity is the increase in the holding of cash or of assets that are very near to cash. From Table 65 we take the following figures of personal holdings:

	£ *m.*
Cash	2,520
Savings bank deposits	2,876
Other 'national savings' securities	2,450
Shares and deposits in building societies and co-operative societies	2,072
	9,918

Nearly 25 per cent. of all personal assets were held in these very highly liquid forms. The war also left many companies and other institutions in a very liquid position with an abnormal proportion of their assets in cash or short-dated bonds.

Finally, there is the technical banking aspect of liquidity. The banks make a conventional distinction between liquid and illiquid assets in which cash, call-money, and bills are regarded as liquid. It has become customary for the banks to maintain these items at a minimum ratio to deposits of 30 per cent., and, provided that the actual ratio is reasonably close to the minimum, the central bank can influence the lending policy of the commercial banks through operations designed to affect the volume of their liquid assets. During most of the post-war period, however, this control has been impaired for two reasons. First the floating debt has been so large that the banks' actual holding of liquid assets has usually been well above the minimum; and, secondly, the banks have held so many very short-dated government securities that they have been able to replenish their technically liquid assets at very little cost, on the rare occasions when this has been necessary, by selling bonds or refusing to convert maturing issues.

The high degree of liquidity in the post-war economy complicated the task of controlling inflation but it did have the effect of mitigating the rise in the yields on government stock that would have been a natural consequence of the growth of the debt in relation to other forms of asset. The new debt created during and shortly after the war was absorbed at moderate rates of interest partly because the growth of liquid assets created new demands from monetary institutions; partly because private savings were coming to the capital market largely through life-assurance companies and pension funds which traditionally held a substantial part of their funds in gilt-edged stocks; and partly because of the skill of the authorities in devising types of borrowing tailored to the special needs of different groups of persons and institutions.

During the past few years, however, the gilt-edged market has come under two kinds of pressure, both connected with inflation. The rise in prices and in money incomes has been proceeding faster than the growth of liquid assets, so that the real value of the stock of liquid assets has been falling. At the same time, investors have become increasingly conscious of the disadvantage of fixed-interest stocks at a time of rising prices. The public debt has remained abnormally large in relation to the total value of property, but the circumstances which, during and immediately after the war, created an abnormal demand for it, have largely disappeared. The result has been a period of high long-term interest rates unprecedented since the creation of the first Consols in the middle of the eighteenth century.

During most of the nineteen-fifties high long-term interest rates were in line with the general aims of monetary policy, and it was excessive liquidity that presented the main monetary problem. Effective liquidity has now been considerably reduced partly by the efforts of the monetary authorities but mainly as a result of inflation. It may be, however, that the general economic position will require lower interest rates in the future and, so long as fixed interest government obligations form so large a part of private property, it may be very difficult to bring rates down without again raising liquidity and risking a recurrence of the difficulties of the early nineteen-fifties.

This is the purely monetary dilemma created by the present structure of property, but there are also wider issues involved.

Where an individual or a small group of individuals directly own real assets, the owners exercise a threefold function. In creating and maintaining the asset, they are foregoing the opportunity of current consumption, and so supplying the 'waiting' or 'abstinence' as it has been variously called that is necessary for capital accumulation. They also, themselves, are responsible for the management of their asset, and they accept the risks which are involved in the ownership of any real asset and especially in the ownership of business assets.

The joint-stock company has done much to separate these three functions; management is put into the hands of specialists who seldom own more than a small fraction of the companies' shares; the supplying of capital is performed by the shareholders in general, but the risk-taking is concentrated on the holders of the ordinary shares (which represent about three-quarters of the total capital of all companies). Public ownership has carried the process still further, for here the risk is covered by government guarantee, but there is still a real sense in which the holder of stock issued by a public corporation can be regarded as supplying capital. Even this concept, however, becomes very strained when one passes from the stock of public corporations to the national debt itself. Here, of course, there is no real asset out of the earnings of which interest is paid or redemption provided for, and the debt is simply a claim on the general revenue of the government.

Some borrowing and lending takes place even in very primitive societies but, until quite recently, financial claims have formed only a minor part of property rights and the typical form of ownership has been that in which the owner was the direct holder of a real asset. Now directly owned real assets form less than one-fifth of private net worth; the equity interest in companies forms rather less than a quarter, and more than half consists of fixed interest obligations of the public sector. This represents a revolution which raises problems for the social philosopher as well as for the economist.

BIBLIOGRAPHY

Government and other Official Publications

Cmd. or Cmnd. = Command No.
H.C. = House of Commons Paper No.

ADVANCES TO ALLIED AND OTHER FOREIGN GOVERNMENTS:

Czechoslovakia	Treaty	Series No.	61, 1949,	Cmd.	7798.
France	,,	,,	57, 1946,	,,	6988.
Germany	,,	,,	2, 1953,	,,	8782.
Netherlands	,,	,,	17, 1948,	,,	7358.
Poland	,,	,,	44, 1947,	,,	7148.
Soviet Union	,,	,,	1, 1948,	,,	7297.
Turkey	,,	,,	4, 1940,	,,	6165.

ANNUAL ABSTRACT OF STATISTICS, Nos. 89 (1952)–92 (1955).

ASSURANCE BUSINESS, Summary statements of, deposited with the Board of Trade during 1953, 1954, and 1955.

BANK OF ENGLAND. United Kingdom Overseas Investments 1953, 1954, and 1955.

Census of 1951.

CENTRAL STATISTICAL OFFICE. National Income and Expenditure (Blue Book), 1953, 1954, 1955.

—— Studies in Official Statistics No. 3. *National Income Statistics, Sources and Methods.* H.M.S.O., London, 1956.

CHARITABLE TRUSTS. *Report of the Committee on the Law and Practice Relating to Charitable Trusts.* Nathan Committee 1952, Cmd. 8710.

CHARITY COMMISSIONERS FOR ENGLAND AND WALES. Annual Reports:
101st—1953.
102nd—1954.
103rd—1955.

CIVIL APPROPRIATION ACCOUNTS. Classes I–V, VI–X, 1952–3, 1953–4, 1954–5.

COUNTY COURTS. Account of the Transactions.... Also the Account of the National Debt Commissioners in respect of . . . the County Courts Funds Investment Accounts 1952, 1953, 1954.

CROWN LANDS, Abstract Account of the Commissioners: 1952–3, H.C. 61.
1953–4, H.C. 42.
1954–5, H.C. 171.

Economic Survey: 1952, Cmd. 8509.
1953, Cmd. 8800.
1954, Cmd. 9108.
1955, Cmd. 9412.
1957, Cmnd. 394.

Economic Trends.

Finance Accounts of the United Kingdom: 1952–3, H.C. 191.
1953–4, H.C. 197.
1954–5, H.C. 8.

Finance and Industry, Reports of Committee on, 1931. Cmd. 3897.

Friendly Societies, Reports of Chief Registrar 1952–5.
Part 1. General.
Part 2. Friendly Societies.
Part 3. Industrial and Provident Societies.
Part 4. Trade Unions.
Part 5. Building Societies.

Hospital Endowments Fund Accounts: 1952–3, H.C. 35.
1953–4, H.C. 2.
1954–5, H.C. 153.

Housing in Britain. Central Office of Information, Reference Division, August 1954.

Housing and Local Government—Annual Reports of Ministry:
1950/1–4, Cmd. 9559.
1954–5, Cmd. 9876.
Houses—the next step: 1953, Cmd. 8996.

Inland Revenue—Annual Reports of Her Majesty's Commissioners:
96th Report 1952–3, Cmd. 9030.
97th „ 1953–4, Cmd. 9351.
98th „ 1954–5, Cmd. 9667.

Irish Land Purchase Fund Accounts: 1952–3, H.C. 37.
1953–4, H.C. 283.
1954–5, H.C. 119.

Local Financial Returns (Scotland): 1952–3, 62nd Report.
1953–4, 63rd Report.
1954–5, 64th Report.

Local Government Financial Statistics—England and Wales: 1952–3, 1953–4, 1954–5.

Local Loans Fund Accounts: 1952–3, H.C. 125.
1953–4, H.C. 80.
1954–5, H.C. 154.

Ministry of Housing and Local Government. *Rates and Rateable Values 1955–6* and Supplement showing Rateable Values and number of Hereditaments in the new valuation lists, which came into force on 1 April 1956.

MINISTRY OF HOUSING AND LOCAL GOVERNMENT. *Rent Control—Statistical Information*, 1956, Cmnd. 17.

Monthly Digest of Statistics.

NATIONAL DEBT RETURN: 1953, Cmd. 8975.
1954, Cmd. 9297.
1955, Cmd. 9621.

NATIONAL INSURANCE FUNDS, ETC., Accounts: 1952–3, H.C. 121.
1953–4, H.C. 107.
1954–5, H.C. 230.

NATIONAL LAND FUND ACCOUNTS: 1952–3, H.C. 269.
1953–4, H.C. 227.
1954–5, H.C. 44.

NATIONAL SAVINGS COMMITTEE, *The Public and National Savings*, 1948.

OCCUPATIONAL PENSION SCHEMES—Government Actuary, 1958.

OLD AGE, *Report of the Committee on the Economic and Financial Problems of the Provision for Old Age* (Phillips Committee), 1954, Cmd. 9333.

POST OFFICE Commercial Accounts and Balance Sheets: 1952–3, H.C. 21.
1953–4, H.C. 299.
1954–5, H.C. 142.

POST OFFICE SAVINGS BANK ACCOUNTS, 1952, 1953, 1954, 1955.

PUBLIC CORPORATIONS:

BRITISH BROADCASTING CORPORATION Annual Report and Account:
1952–3, Cmd. 8928.
1953–4, Cmd. 9269.
1954–5, Cmd. 9803.

BRITISH ELECTRICITY AUTHORITY Report and Accounts:
5th, 1952–3, H.C. 251.
6th, 1953–4, H.C. 234.
7th, 1954–5, H.C. 74.

BRITISH EUROPEAN AIRWAYS Reports and Accounts: 1952–3, H.C. 277.
1953–4, H.C. 265.
1954–5, H.C. 88.

BRITISH OVERSEAS AIRWAYS CORPORATION: 1952–3, H.C. 278.
1953–4, H.C. 266.
1954–5, H.C. 89.

BRITISH TRANSPORT COMMISSION Annual Report and Accounts:
5th, 1952, H.C. 190.
6th, 1953, H.C. 268.
7th, 1954, H.C. 20.
8th, 1955, H.C. 290.

CABLE AND WIRELESS LTD. Accounts: 31 March 1953, Cmd. 8913.
31 March 1954, Cmd. 9234.
31 March 1955, Cmd. 9546.

COLONIAL DEVELOPMENT CORPORATION Report and Accounts:
1952, H.C. 158.
1953, H.C. 148.
1954, H.C. 113.

GAS COUNCIL Report and Accounts: 4th, 1952–3, H.C. 241.
5th, 1953–4, H.C. 262.
6th, 1954–5, H.C. 86.

INDEPENDENT TELEVISION AUTHORITY Annual Report and Accounts: 31 March 1955, H.C. 123.

IRON AND STEEL CORPORATION OF GREAT BRITAIN Report and Accounts: 1951–2, H.C. 198.

IRON AND STEEL HOLDING AND REALIZATION AGENCY Report and Statement of Accounts:
13 July 1954–30 September 1954, H.C. 7.
1 October 1954–30 September 1955, H.C. 152.

NATIONAL COAL BOARD Annual Report and Statement of Accounts:
1952, H.C. 157.
1953, H.C. 160.
1954, H.C. 1.
1955, H.C. 263.

NATIONAL DOCK LABOUR BOARD Annual Report, 1952.

NATIONAL FILM FINANCE CORPORATION Annual Report and Accounts:
31 March 1953, Cmd. 8816.
31 March 1954, Cmd. 9166.
31 March 1955, Cmd. 9751.

NATIONAL RESEARCH DEVELOPMENT CORPORATION—Report and Statement of Accounts: 30 June 1953, H.C. 23.
30 June 1954, H.C. 27.
30 June 1955, H.C. 232.

NEW TOWNS ACTS 1946–53 Accounts: 31 Mar. 1953, H.C. 133.
31 Mar. 1954, H.C. 137.
31 Mar. 1955, H.C. 285.

NORTH OF SCOTLAND HYDRO-ELECTRIC BOARD Report and Accounts:
1952, H.C. 99.
1954, H.C. 54.
1955, H.C. 193.

OVERSEAS FOOD CORPORATION Report and Accounts:
31 Mar. 1953, H.C. 30.
31 Mar. 1954, H.C. 296.
31 Mar. 1955, H.C. 195.

RAW COTTON COMMISSION Annual Report and Statement of Accounts:
31 Aug. 1953, H.C. 172.
31 Aug. 1954, H.C. 13.

SCOTTISH SPECIAL HOUSING ASSOCIATION LTD. Annual Digest:
31 Mar. 1953, 6th.
31 Mar. 1956, 9th.

UNITED KINGDOM ATOMIC ENERGY AUTHORITY: 1st Report, 19 July 1954–31 Mar. 1955, H.C. 95.

PUBLIC TRUSTEES OFFICE Annual Reports: 1952–3, 45th.
1953–4, 46th.
1954–5, 47th.

PUBLIC WORKS LOANS BOARD Annual Reports: 1952–3, 78th.
1953–4, 79th.
1954–5, 80th.

RESISTRAR-GENERAL—Decennial Supplement, 1951 Census of Great Britain. 1 per cent. sample tables.

ROYAL COMMISSION ON TAXATION. Memorandum of the British Bankers' Association to the Royal Commission on the Taxation of Profits and Income, July 1951, June 1952.

STATISTICAL DIGEST OF THE WAR. *History of the Second World War*. U.K. Civil Series.

TRADING ACCOUNT AND BALANCE-SHEETS:
1952–3, Vols. 1 and 11, H.C. 22 and 22.1.
1953–4, H.C. 298.
1954–5, H.C. 138.

TRUSTEE SAVINGS BANK ACCOUNTS: 20 Nov. 1953.
" 1954.
" 1955.

UNIVERSITY GRANTS COMMITTEE—Returns from Universities and University Colleges in Receipt of Treasury Grant 1953–4, Cmd. 9477.

WAR DAMAGE (Business and Private Chattels Schemes) Account:
1952–3, H.C. 116.
1954–5, H.C. 179.

WAR DAMAGE (Land and Buildings) Account: 1952–3, H.C. 73.
1955–6, H.C. 7.

WAR RISKS (COMMODITIES) Insurance Fund Accounts, 1943–4, H.C. 51.

Other Publications

BACON, F. W., BENJAMIN, B., and ELPHINSTONE, M. D. W. *The Growth of Pension Rights and their Impact on the National Economy*, Institute of Actuaries and the Faculty of Actuaries, London, 1953.

BALOGH, T. *Studies in Financial Organisation*, National Institute of Economic and Social Research, Cambridge University Press, London, 1947.

BEVERIDGE, W. H., and WELLS, A. (Eds.). *The Evidence for Voluntary Action*, Allen & Unwin, London, 1949.

BOWLEY, MARION. *Housing and the State, 1919–1944*, Allen & Unwin, London, 1947.

CAMPION, H. *Public and Private Property in Great Britain*, Oxford University Press, London, 1939.

CHARITABLE TRUSTS. *Reports of a Survey of Charitable Trusts in Great Britain—providing funds for the accommodation, care and comfort of old people*, Nuffield Foundation, 1947.

CITRINE, N. A. *Trade Union Law*, Stevens, London, 1950.

CO-OPERATIVE UNION LTD. *A Review of Co-operative Statistics*, Manchester, 1953, 1954, 1955, 1956.

CUTHBERTSON, J. R. 'Property Holding Habits of Individuals', *The Banker*, vol. ci, nos. 330 and 331, July and Aug. 1953.

DUNNING, J. H. *American Investment in British Manufacturing Industry*, Allen & Unwin, London, 1958.

HARRIS, RALPH and SELDON, ARTHUR, *Hire Purchase in a Free Society*, Institute of Economic Affairs, London, 1958.

INSTITUTE OF MUNICIPAL TREASURERS AND ACCOUNTANTS. *Research Study—the investments of Local Authorities.*

—— *Return of Outstanding Debt*, 1952, 1954, 1956.

INTEREST AND DIVIDENDS UPON SECURITIES QUOTED ON THE LONDON STOCK EXCHANGE. Council of the Stock Exchange, London, 1950–4, 1955, 1956.

JONES, E. GWEN and NEVIN, E. 'The British National Debt', I, *Economica*, vol. xxiv, no. 95, Aug. 1957; II, ibid., vol. xxiv, no. 96, Nov. 1957.

KING, W. T. C. 'The Return to Bill Dealing', *The Banker*, vol. ci, no. 331, Aug. 1953.

—— 'Restoring Flexible Money', ibid., no. 333, Oct. 1953.

—— 'Profits in Lombard Street', ibid., no. 342, July 1954.

—— 'Lombard Street Takes the Strain', ibid., no. 354, July 1955.

—— 'Should the Bill Tender be Freed', ibid., no. 355, Aug. 1955.

LANGLEY, KATHLEEN M. 'The Distribution of Capital in Private Hands in 1936–8 and 1946–7, Part I. The Distribution of Capital According to the Number of Persons', *Bulletin of the Oxford University Institute of Statistics*, vol. 12, no. 12, Dec. 1950.

—— Part II. 'The Distribution of Capital According to Amount of Capital', ibid., vol. 13, no. 2, Feb. 1951.

—— 'An Analysis of the Asset Structure of Estates, 1900–1949', ibid., vol. 13, no. 10, Oct. 1951.

—— 'The Distribution of Private Capital, 1950–51', ibid., vol. 16, no. 1, Jan. 1954.

LEES, D. S. 'Public Departments and Cheap Money 1932–8', *Economica*, vol. xxii, no. 85, Feb. 1955.

LYDALL, H. F. 'A Pilot Survey of Income and Savings', *Bulletin of the Oxford University Institute of Statistics*, vol. 13, no. 9, Sept. 1951.

—— 'Liquid Asset Holdings in Oxford', ibid., vol. 14, no. 3, Mar. 1952.

—— 'Personal Savings and Its Determinants in the Light of the Oxford Survey', ibid., vol. 14, no. 7, July 1952.

—— 'National Survey of Personal Incomes and Savings', ibid., vol. 14, Nos. 11 and 12, Nov. and Dec. 1952. *Also* vol. 15, nos. 2 and 3, Feb. and Mar. 1953; vol. 15, nos. 6 and 7, June and July 1953; vol. 15, nos. 10 and 11, Oct. and Nov. 1953.

—— 'The Methods of the Savings Survey', ibid., vol. 16, nos. 7 and 8, July and Aug. 1954.

LYSONS, A. 'The Sources of Finance for Industry and Commerce in Great Britain since the War', *Bankers' Magazine*, vol. clxviii, no. 1326, Sept. 1954.

MACRAE, N. *The London Capital Market*, Staples Press Ltd., London, 1955.

MORGAN, E. V. *Studies in British Financial Policy 1914–25*, Macmillan, London, 1952.

NATIONAL INSTITUTE OF ECONOMIC AND SOCIAL RESEARCH. *Finance of Public Companies*, 1953.

—— A Classified List of Large Companies engaged in British Industry, 1956.

—— *Company Income and Finance 1949–53*, Cambridge University Press, London, 1956.

NEVIN, E. 'Some facts about "tap" Treasury Bills', *The Banker*, vol. civ, no. 348, Jan. 1955.

—— *The Problem of the National Debt*, University of Wales Press, Cardiff, 1954.

PAISH, F. W. *The Post-War Financial Problem and Other Essays*, Macmillan, London, 1950.

PEMKER AND BOYLE. *British Government Securities in the 20th Century* (private publication), London, 1950.

PENSION FUNDS AND EQUITY MARKETS. *Investors' Chronicle*, 151, 1955.

REDDAWAY, W. B. 'Housing Problems', *Three Banks Review*, No. 23, Sept. 1954.

REDFERN, P. 'Net Investment in Fixed Assets in the United Kingdom, 1938–1953', *Journal of the Royal Statistical Society*, Series A, vol. 118, part 2, 1955.

SARGENT, J. R. 'A Rent, Dividend and Interest Account for 1948', *Bulletin of the Oxford University Institute of Statistics*, vol. 14, no. 1, Jan. 1952.

SAUNDERS, C. T. 'Some Problems in the Estimation of Personal Savings and Investment', *Review of Economic Studies*, vol. xxii, no. 58, 1954–55.

SIMON, E. D. *Rebuilding Britain—a 20 year plan*, Gollancz, London, 1945.

THE ASSOCIATION OF SUPERANNUATION AND PENSION FUNDS, *Statistics*, London, 1956.

'The National Debt Examined', *Midland Bank Review*, Aug. 1953.

'The Size and Shape of the National Debt', ibid., Feb. 1950.

Yearbooks, &c.

British Bankers Association Year Book.
Building Societies Year Book.
Chitty's Annual Statutes.
Church of England Year Book.
Family Welfare Association—*Annual Register and Digest.*
Public General Acts and Measures.
Stock Exchange Yearbook.
Whitaker's Almanack.

INDEX

QUEEN MARY COLLEGE
LIBRARY
MILE END ROAD
LONDON. E.1.

PRINTED IN GREAT BRITAIN
AT THE UNIVERSITY PRESS, OXFORD
BY VIVIAN RIDLER
PRINTER TO THE UNIVERSITY